2: PERSPECTIVES IN CRITICISM

PERSPECTIVES IN CRITICISM

2:

Solomon Fishman

The Disinherited of Art

WRITER AND BACKGROUND

UNIVERSITY OF CALIFORNIA PRESS
Berkeley and Los Angeles
1953

University of California Press
Berkeley and Los Angeles, California

Cambridge University Press
London, England

Manufactured in the United States of America
by the University of California Printing Department
Designed by Ward Ritchie

Preface

THE SUBJECT matter of these essays is literary criticism. My aim is not to make a survey of modern criticism, to explain it, or to evaluate the work of individual critics. I wish only to examine a single aspect of contemporary literary thought—speculation concerning the impact of culture on literature.

At one time I had hoped to deal with this subject in a systematic manner; if not exhaustively, then at least in a continuous sequence; to set forth certain premises, to examine the available materials, and to draw pertinent conclusions. My initial efforts convinced me that the subject was intractable to a systematic study, whereas it did lend itself more readily to treatment in a series of essays. These essays, then, are meant to form an integral whole. Each of them was composed with the central topic in mind—the relations of literature and culture.

Although I limit my discussion to contemporary criticism, the topic itself is certainly not new. If we exchange "culture" for "society," we have a subject that has occupied critics continuously since the eighteenth century. Although our own century has witnessed a great increase in the production of criticism and literary scholarship, it has not been a period marked by revolutionary changes in literary theory. Yet gradual changes have occurred. Some of the ideas of a century ago, or even a generation ago, have undergone drastic modification. Neither "society" nor "literature" has quite the same connotation it had formerly. What is more important, we are not so certain that the connections between them can be drawn as clearly as was formerly believed.

The close, careful textual studies in which contemporary criticism excels have made us conscious of the almost infinite complexity of literary works. Recent work in history, sociology, and anthropology has altered previous generalizations about the nature of society. The expansion of knowledge is reason enough for reopening the question of literature in relation to society.

General literary theory has been one of my chief concerns, but I have, for purposes of illustration, confined myself to contemporary American criticism, and only to the part of it that deals with American writing. I do not maintain that this is either the most interesting or the most important part of our criticism, for some of our ablest critics have been as much occupied with foreign works as with native ones. Since the field of inspection had to be narrowed, I have concentrated on what appears to be most relevant to the main topic.

I do think that this topic has assumed more importance in our own literary thinking than in European criticism. It is in a way a special American subject. It makes itself felt nearly every time an American critic discusses an American writer or work. I think also that whenever it has been insisted on too strenuously it has lessened the critic's capacity for judging literary works. But nothing is served by ignoring the question altogether or by pretending that the relationship between literature and society, if it does exist, is irrelevant to the critic's task. The real problem is rather to discover, if we can, where information about society hinders and where it furthers the critic's task. The solution is more likely to be found in a discriminating practice of criticism than in theoretical speculations; the discrepancy between the idea of the literary work of art as an autonomous whole and that of the work as a phenomenon bounded, like other human products, by space and time is not easily resolved in philosophic terms.

The special fascination that social questions have for American critics is explained by certain singularities of our literary culture and, indeed, of our culture as a whole. I have suggested in one of these essays ("Literature and

Society: Two Versions") that "culture" rather than "society" is the more useful term for purposes of literary discussion. "Culture" is, of course, the more difficult term. In lay usage it can be made so inclusive as to contain almost everything. But lack of precision may actually be an advantage in indicating the relationship of a literary work to its environment if it serves only to prevent oversimplification. In this context "culture" is actually the more accurate term, since it encompasses the writer's artistic and intellectual milieu, which is just as important for criticism as his material and moral milieu.

The first essay ("Gestures of Rejection") does not stress literary theory as much as the others. It deals with a prominent trait in American literature of the past century—the writer's sense of alienation from his culture. By "alienation" is meant the writer's realization that his environment is somehow inimical to his vocation. The term itself is perhaps unfortunate, suggesting as it does current professional jargon, but I have not discovered a better one.

The third, fourth, and fifth essays are devoted to literary theory relating not so much to individual works as to the whole body of American literature. Questions of literary nationalism, regionalism, and internationalism are by no means peculiar to American criticism, but they do not seem to have elsewhere the same urgency they do here. The explanation lies in an unprecedented situation that is a consequence of the greatly accelerated movement of history in the past two centuries. The United States has become the dominant force in the world before we have had time to recognize and know our culture.

In literature the cultural situation was complicated by our colonial beginnings. So long as awareness of a colonial past survives, any culture will harbor a sense of inferiority. Though our literature has by now acquired sufficient bulk and importance to assure its status as a national literature, we are still sensitive on the score of provinciality. I think we are about to outgrow our awkwardness in the presence of this subject, but the touchiness still exists in certain areas.

It is present, for example, in aggressive literary nationalism. I have tried to deal objectively with the important matter of nationality in literature in spite of a strong bias in this quarter. I feel that literary nationalists have been most guilty of misapplying social information to literature. Instead of pursuing linguistic investigations—the significance of idiom and speech rhythms in our letters, for instance—they have for the most part attempted to establish criteria for a national literature on the writer's handling of social experience alone.

The habit of regarding national culture as the normal milieu of the writer is disputed by two different points of view. The regionalist doctrine raises doubt whether the United States possesses a homogeneous culture. The regionalists believe that distinct cultures in any form that can be significant or useful for the writer exist only at the regional level. Regionalism, of course, covers a wide variety of opinion on both literature and society. For the student of criticism the ideas of the Southern agrarians have extraordinary interest. Their social theory is founded upon the idea of an organic culture based upon the soil of a relatively limited geographical area. Their literary interests, however, are anything but local. In criticism they advocate the notion of universal standards, and their own criticism is rigorous in excluding social and historical considerations. I have tried to demonstrate the essential connection between their social ideas and their literary theories.

The nationalist view of literature as a product of social experience is challenged by those who regard intellectual culture as intrinsically international and autonomous concerning the principal activities of society. According to this view, American literature shares the tradition of literature in English and participates in the broader tradition of European letters reaching back to Homer. The subject of divided loyalties occurs frequently in our writing; in the essay "The Transatlantic Element" I have tried to trace its origins and to point out some of the stresses it has produced in criticism. My own point of view here is pluralistic. We cannot justly assess the achievement of American writers if we insist on a standard based on fidelity to a strictly native tradition.

The last essay in the series ("The Shape of Democratic Art") discusses the status of literary art in contemporary culture. The critic is not strictly obliged to involve himself in this matter, though he must eventually come to grips with it if he is at all concerned with the contemporary scene. Although I have again confined myself to American writing, my analysis leans heavily on the views of a European sociologist, Karl Mannheim, who possessed great insight into the relations of modern intellectual activity and modern social organization.

These essays are not offered as a complete guide through the intricacies of a vast and difficult subject. Intricacy and complexity ought to be recognized as such where they actually exist. To the reader who is disappointed by the absence of both positions and conclusions, I should say that these essays are cautionary rather than positive; their purpose is to detect and to censure attitudes that deflect us from viewing the literary work in its integrity or detract from its innate complexity.

It is perhaps regrettable that a book discussing literary criticism should convey so little of the flavor of literature. It is guilty of a fault I have not hesitated to point out in others—absorption in extraliterary matters to a point where the true object of literary studies, the work itself is lost sight of. I hope the reader will perceive that I have been demonstrating by precept rather than by example.

For permission to quote copyrighted material, I wish to express my thanks to:

Appleton-Century-Crofts, Inc., for quotations from *Spokesmen*, by T. K. Whipple.

Newton Arvin for quotations from "The Democratic Tradition in American Letters," in *The Writer in a Changing World*, edited by H. Hart.

Felix S. Cohen for quotations from *Reason and Nature*, by Morris R. Cohen.

Columbia University Press for quotations from: *The Roots of American Loyalty*, by Merle Curti; and *The Psychological Frontiers of Society*, by A. Kardiner and R. Linton.

J. M. Dent and Sons for quotations from: *The Flowering of New England*, by Van Wyck Brooks; and *New England: Indian Summer*, by Van Wyck Brooks.

Bernard De Voto for quotations from *Mark Twain's America*.

Dial Press for quotations from "Avant-Garde and Kitsch," by Clement Greenberg, in *The Partisan Reader*, edited by William Phillips and Philip Rahv.

E. P. Dutton and Company, Inc., for quotations from: *The Flowering of New England*, by Van Wyck Brooks; *New England: Indian Summer*, by Van Wyck Brooks; and *Three Essays on America*, by Van Wyck Brooks.

Harcourt, Brace and Company, Inc., for quotations from: *Portrait of the Artist as an American*, by Matthew Josephson; *On Native Grounds*, by Alfred Kazin; *Man and Society*, by Karl Mannheim; *Faith for Living*, by Lewis Mumford; *Main Currents in American Thought*, by Vernon L. Parrington; *The Roots of American Culture*, by Constance Rourke; and *Civilization in the United States*, by Harold E. Stearns.

Harper and Brothers for quotations from: *The Growth of American Thought*, by Merle Curti; *Criticism and Fiction*, by William Dean Howells; *Hawthorne*, by Henry James; *Expression in America*, by Ludwig Lewisohn; *The Wind Blew from the East*, by Ferner Nuhn; and *Literary Opinion in America*, by Morton D. Zabel.

Harvard University Press for quotations from: *Ideas in America*, by Howard Mumford Jones; and *Three Philosophical Poets*, by George Santayana.

D. C. Heath and Company for quotations from the foreword, by Henry Seidel Canby, to *The American Reader*, by Claude M. Simpson and Allan Nevins.

Granville Hicks for quotations from *The Great Tradition*.

Henry Holt and Company, Inc., for quotations from *The Question of Henry James*, by F. W. Dupee.

Houghton Mifflin Company for quotations from: *Rousseau and Romanticism*, by Irving Babbitt; and *The Discovery of Europe*, by Philip Rahv.

Lincoln Kirstein for quotations from "Henry James in the World," by Edna Kenton, in *Hound and Horn*, April-May, 1934.

Alfred A. Knopf, Inc., for quotations from *The Armed Vision*, by Stanley Edgar Hyman; and *A Book of Prefaces*, by H. L. Mencken.

Liveright Publishing Corporation for quotations from *Our America*, by Waldo Frank (copyright, 1947, by Waldo Frank).

The Macmillan Company for quotations from: *A History of English Literature*, by E. Legouis and L. Cazamian; *Art and Society*, by Herbert Read; and *Literary History of the United States*, edited by R. E. Spiller, W. Thorp, T. H. Johnson, and H. S. Canby.

The editor of the *Nation* for quotations from "Individualism and the American Writer," by Newton Arvin, in the *Nation*, October 14, 1931.

New Directions for quotations from "The Madonna of the Future," by Henry James, in *Stories of Writers and Artists*, edited by F. O. Matthiessen.

The publisher of the *New Republic* for quotations from "America, Listen to Your Own," by D. H. Lawrence, in the *New Republic*, December 15, 1920.

William A. Orton for quotations from *America in Search of Culture*.

Oxford University Press, Inc., for quotations from: *The Achievement of T. S. Eliot*, by F. O. Matthiessen; and *American Renaissance*, by F. O. Matthiessen.

The editors of the *Partisan Review* for quotations from: "Writers and Madness," by William Barrett, in the *Partisan Review*, January-February, 1947; "Dostoevsky's

Underground Man," by William Phillips, in the *Partisan Review*, November-December, 1946; "The Intellectuals' Tradition," by William Phillips, in the *Partisan Review*, November-December, 1941; and "Concerning Tolstoi," by Philip Rahv, in the *Partisan Review*, September-October, 1946.

G. P. Putnam's Sons for quotations from *Art as Experience*, by John Dewey.

Routledge and Kegan Paul, Ltd., for quotations from *Man and Society*, by Karl Mannheim.

The editor of the *Saturday Review of Literature* for quotations from "The American Tradition in Literature," by Henry Seidel Canby, in the *Saturday Review of Literature*, August 31, 1940.

Charles Scribner's Sons for quotations from: *The Liberation of American Literature*, by V. F. Calverton; *The World's Body*, by John Crowe Ransom; and *Reactionary Essays*, by Allen Tate.

Wallace Stegner for quotations from "Regionalism in Art," in the *Delphian Quarterly*, January, 1939.

Alan Swallow for quotations from *In Defense of Reason*, by Yvor Winters, published by The University of Denver Press, 1947.

The University of North Carolina Press for quotations from *The Attack on Leviathan*, by Donald Davidson.

The University of Oklahoma Press for quotations from *Folk-Say I*, by B. A. Botkin.

The Viking Press, Inc., for quotations from: *Exile's Return*, by Malcom Cowley; *Studies in Classic American Literature*, by D. H. Lawrence; and *Black Lamb and Grey Falcon*, by Rebecca West.

Contents

1

Gestures of Rejection

A STRIKING EVENT in the world of letters is the present vogue of contemporary American fiction in France. Among the younger French writers particularly, admiration for Hemingway, Farrell, Caldwell, Steinbeck, and above all, for Faulkner, is said to have assumed the proportions of a literary movement. Some critics there have considered the "Americanization" of French writing as a defection from the proud native literary tradition. On this side of the Atlantic the success of American writing abroad can seem only salutary; yet it does not signify, as some of us have been quick to assume, a reversal of the normal roles of European and American culture, nor an unambiguous tribute to the attainment of full majority by American literature.

The success of American writing in Europe does register at least one important fact; for the first time a whole body of American writing—not merely the work of an individual writer like Cooper or Poe or Emerson or Longfellow, or Jack London or Sinclair Lewis, all of whom won either critical or popular esteem abroad—has been received as a valid and powerful representation of states of mind and emotion common to Western man. American literary critics are entitled to some gratification in this moment, marking the goal of the slow progress of American letters to world status. Furthermore, this is the only body of writing in America for which the critics can take honest credit; it appeared in a period of active, articulate criticism sympathetic to the aims of contemporary writers and devoted to the task of creating a climate favorable to contemporary work.

But has the international reputation of these novelists

1

really been earned by literary merit? Is it not rather their preoccupation with violence and cruelty, with the insupportable tensions between the individual and his environment, that have struck home at a time when the European mind is extraordinarily receptive to images of dissolution? The European reader has brought to them not only his own awareness of the violence done to the human spirit by a hostile, dehumanized world and his own sense of estrangement from that world; he has also read into them more general philosophic and social import than was probably intended. There is a certain irony in the knowledge that the greatness of American literature has been recognized in writing so thoroughly obsessed with the theme of disintegration.

The liaison between contemporary critics and novelists, though closer than in previous eras, is hardly an active alliance. It would be as unjust to give entire credit to the critics for the excellences of contemporary fiction as to tax them with responsibility for its preoccupation with violence. Yet it is not unreasonable to infer that both criticism and imaginative fiction derive power and distinction from awareness of disintegration in modern life. That such awareness is a condition of literary thought in America is not, after all, startling in view of similar matter in European literature of the nineteenth century. Failure to correlate American literary experience with the chief movements of modern thought and the tendency to regard it as a special instance of cultural development account for certain distortions of judgment concerning the relation of American literature to American culture. They explain not only the ambivalence in the American writer's attitude toward his country, but the excesses of guilt and pessimism, idealism and expectation, in our literary criticism.

It must be remembered that American literature is, historically considered, almost entirely modern; even the works of its classic period bear the stigmata of the modern consciousness, among which are a sense of social disintegration, of cultural decadence, and of the widening schism between the individual and his moral and material environment. Granted the affinities of the European and the American intellect, the American writer is probably more susceptible to signs of decadence than his European counterpart. The former's extraordinary sensitivity is neither recent nor eccentric; nor is it, as is popularly assumed, largely derivative. This sensitivity already existed in the nineteenth century, when the distance separating European and American culture was far greater than now. In the nineteenth century, American society, it is true, appeared anything but decadent. Much of its literature also was animated by vigor and optimism. But in the latter half of the century the writer was as likely to be repelled as attracted by his society. The spectacle of material health sometimes intensified his estimate of its spiritual shortcomings and confirmed his isolation from its purposes.

In the decades after the Civil War, what had been a disturbing but indeterminate premonition of the dislocations of modern life was transformed into much more articulate statements of resignation, protest, or pessimism. Alfred Kazin predicates the homogeneity of American writing since 1870 on a single hypothesis: "The greatest fact about our modern American writing is the writers' absorption in every last detail of their American world together with their deep and subtle alienation from it. There is a terrible estrangement in this writing, a nameless yearning for a world no one ever really possessed, that rises above the skills our writers have mastered."[1] Though the effect upon criticism was somewhat delayed, an attitude so pervasive and deeply felt in the literary atmosphere can hardly have left the critic untouched. His awareness of alienation as an element in American letters and his own involvement in the American world are integral features of the over-all literary sensibility. His alienation is not easily distinguishable from the novelist's or poet's, particularly when

3

critic and poet are the same person or when the critic turns apologist for his contemporaries. The critic's experience, however, is complicated by his mediate position between literature and society; often he is alienated not only from his environment but also in subtle way from the literature he advocates.

This situation, wherein the critic's attitude toward American society impinges so sharply on his evaluation of its literature, is normal in an era when aesthetic certainties are as difficult to come by as moral or theological certainties. It is doubtful whether criticism can be governed by aesthetic standards unless it functions within a relatively stable cultural framework or unless, as has happened in our time, the critic arrives at his own certainties by a deliberate act of will, thereby defying the disbelief of the age. American criticism of this century, whether it be sociological or aesthetic, relativistic or absolute in principle, has been implicated in cultural considerations to an unprecedented degree; and these have been provoked mainly by the critics' profound disaffection with their native culture.

To ascribe the literary climate of our era to a single, dominant impulse is rash. Important variations and exceptions exist. The 1930's especially witnessed much shifting of allegiances: conversions, defections, radical revisions of belief. At the time it seemed that literary morale was undergoing a thorough reformation from intransigent skepticism to positive faith, and that American writing, hitherto nonconforming, was on the verge of a new affirmative phase. The effects of the "political" decade do not now seem to have been conclusive; at least they do not justify a thorough reconsideration of the quality of twentieth-century American letters.

Although I hesitate to assign arbitrary limits, this literary era may be regarded as spanning the interval between the First and Second World wars. The era encompasses two generations, one mature by 1914, the other approaching maturity during the 'twenties. The

4

earlier one was, as Malcolm Cowley has said, the first real generation in American letters, the first to exhibit a homogeneous sensibility. Its salient characteristic was a youthfulness conspicuous in its rejection of prevailing values and attitudes. In this the literary movement of the 'twenties resembles the romantic revolt of the previous century. To designate it as a rebirth of romanticism would be incorrect, however. Its modes of rejection were less personal; its disillusionment was violent, persistent, and (in the first phase) unrelieved by romantic optimism; it failed to discover the consolations of landscape or memory.

The key to this new cycle of American literature is the term "alienation." It includes a whole constellation of attitudes associated with the literary 'twenties: isolation, individualism, bohemianism, dissidence, rejection, rebellion, disillusion, pessimism, defeat, decadence, disintegration, escape, exile. Alienation, in brief, implies a centrifugal impulse, the detachment of the particle from the mass. The response to any given situation, however, is rarely absolute acceptance or rejection; upon closer scrutiny each usually discloses a mixture of positive and negative attitudes. Hence the areas of ambivalence in the writing of this period which belie its apparent homogeneity.

The most palpable, though not necessarily the most significant, evidence of alienation was the mass migration of American writers to Europe in the decade after the First World War. The pattern of migration had, to be sure, been fairly normal for nearly a century; this time it was obvious that the migration of American writers and artists to Europe was no pedagogical interlude in the style of the Grand Tour, but a traumatic symptom. The writer now wished actually to sever relations with his native culture in order to discover a more propitious cultural setting. Granted that voluntary expatriation always indicates an underlying maladjustment, the motive for individual acts of expatriation was various.

5

For some the act was a deliberate choice based on vocational considerations, primarily the belief that a writer could better realize his powers where an active intellectual and aesthetic tradition continued to operate. For others it was mainly an attempt to evade the constricting effect of American manners and morals in a more congenial environment, one that allowed the individual greater scope for self-development and self-expression in both art and life.

A clue to the difference was the traveler's goal. If it was London, he was probably seeking an ancestral home, wishing to affiliate with a continuing tradition, even though by now attenuated; if it was Paris, he probably wished to liberate himself from the cramp of hateful social, ethical, and intellectual surroundings, to cut bonds of attachment already frayed and to dramatize his sense of isolation. The most notable writer in the first category, and perhaps the only one who fully grasped the cultural implications of his act, is T. S. Eliot. Eliot's identification with the society and culture of his adopted country has been so thorough that he can no longer be classed simply as an American writer.

Eliot's career might serve to illustrate a state of mind characteristic of the contemporary American writer; but his work, particularly his criticism, does not explicitly illuminate the American writer's cultural predicament. Apprehending alienation as the central flaw in the modern consciousness, he has considered its pertinence to Western culture as a whole rather than its specifically American features. The great specialist in the American features is Van Wyck Brooks, whose resistance to the magnetic pull of Europe was as deliberate as Eliot's expatriation. Brooks's early essays, *America's Coming of Age* (1915) and *Letters and Leadership* (1918), inaugurated a movement that has not yet subsided. They are not, strictly considered, literary criticism, but a combination of cultural criticism and literary manifesto. Intended as irritants in an era of complacency, their manner was

6

frankly hortatory. They were addressed to American writers.

Although these essays have now lost much of their pertinence and force, they still have great historical interest. They managed to articulate the unformulated dissatisfactions of the postwar period and organize its rebellious impulses. Two decades later, when Brooks was uneasy about the brash iconoclasm of these essays, he attributed their acerbity to the time spirit. Yet they helped create that time spirit, if only by defining it. They laid heavy stress on the formative influence of national culture in art, particularly its effect upon the artist's personality. The divergence between Eliot and Brooks was thus clear from the start: Eliot's early essays abrogated personality as an element in aesthetic discussion; Brooks, however, concentrated on the warping of the writer's personality by his environment. Interest in the writer's psyche, merely adumbrated in Brooks's early essays, was later realized in his full-length studies of Henry James and Mark Twain.

The subject of these essays is the defeat of the American artist by his environment, whose barrenness is ascribed to a schizoid division in the national mind between an unworldly, self-deceptive, official outlook (the residue of a desiccated puritanism) and the actual national morality based on crass utility and money grubbing. Except for Walt Whitman, who confronted the actualities and found in them a "sense of something organic," a national center, American writers were either taken in by the official version or, undeceived by it, took refuge in "diaphanous private worlds of mist and twilight." As a result of this split, "those of our writers who have possessed a vivid personal genius have been paralyzed by the want of a social background, while those who have possessed a vivid social genius have been equally unable to develop their personalities."[2] The failure to create an American literature integrated with national life and culture is emphasized by the contrast

7

with Europe, where the writer acts as a catalyst in his society. "To question and exhilarate the life of one's own people—as Heine and Nietzsche did in Germany, as Matthew Arnold, William Morris and H. G. Wells have done in England—is to bring, not peace, but a sword."[3] The ideal writer accordingly becomes the conscience of his people, an opponent of the *status quo,* who must "overthrow and dissolve" society in order to re-create it.

Brooks's view of the writer's relation to society is ambivalent. His studies of writers victimized by their environment reveal him to be a thoroughgoing determinist. But most determinist literary philosophies, as Harry Levin has observed in "Literature as an Institution" (*Accent,* Spring, 1946), contain an escape clause, generally of the idealist variety. Brooks is no exception: he provides the writer with an apocalyptic role. His ideal writer is not only a representative of the racial norm, "the flower that has an organic connection with the soil from which it springs"; he is also a rebel against his environment, an opponent of social conformity.

It was Brooks's own dissidence in his early writings that struck home. Although these early writings reflected the negativism and the acute irritability of the time, they were not passive or resigned. They called for a bold attack on the problems of American culture and literature, and helped inaugurate a literary mode—critical realism—in which were concentrated the impulses toward rebellion that had been stirring beneath the apparent placidity of the literary scene.

Brooks's radicalism was different from that of his fellow writers in one important respect. Though it proceeded, as did theirs, from a sense of alienation, it contained a conservative core—a profound impulse toward a point of rest—probably more native to his temperament than his nonconformity. At the same time he was urging the writer to attack and expose, he also declared the writer's indispensable attachment to his native soil. The idyllic nationalism of *The Flowering of New England* and the subsequent volumes of his literary history was not, as some critics charged, a betrayal but something that had been implicit in his earlier position. There had been no pride in Brooks's castigation of his culture but only regret. While other writers, impelled by the pang of homelessness, were trying to strike root in foreign cultures, Brooks immersed himself in the American past. What he found there brought about a complete reconciliation; what had once seemed sterile and hostile to artistic production now semed bountiful in its cultural fulfillments and possibilities. It is likewise irrelevant to charge Brooks with abandoning his former standards, since his criteria of excellence had never been aesthetic but had been founded on the idea of literature as social or personal expression. He had demanded that the writer be the voice of his people; his revised judgment of American culture in the nineteenth century inevitably altered his estimate of the literature.

Van Wyck Brooks's importance as an intellectual force is obscured by the current success of the critical school that repudiates the sociological and biographical as well as the nationalist approach to literature. His work, however, forms an accurate index to a large segment of the contemporary literary sensibility. His original thesis—the "ordeal" of the American artist—provided the sole subject of a school of criticism in the 'twenties and, despite Brook's recantation, it possessed sufficient validity to color criticism in the following decade. This criticism emphasized the destructive effect of America upon its creative artists. This point of view was highly subjective. Informed by his own sense of alienation and that of his contemporaries, the critic was inclined to view his situation as universal and to project it into the past. In the new literary histories of the 'twenties and 'thirties the nineteenth century, once classified as an era of democratic progress, now divulged a record of isolation, frustration, failure, and inferiority.

Though the literary activity of the second and third

decades of the twentieth century was marked by great vigor, its vitality was not matched by its temper, which was mainly negative and disillusioned. A possible explanation is that the writer who began his career after 1900 was aware of a cultural void in his immediate past; the post-Civil War slump (as Edmund Wilson has called it) conditioned his outlook on the whole of American literature. In its critical phase the writing of the period after the First World War encompassed attitudes of rejection ranging from recoil and denunciation to conscientious analysis. The median view declared categorically that American life stifled the production of art; it confirmed Brooks's pronouncements on the incompatibility of the artist and the social environment.

The alienation of American writers had in the past exhibited two classic patterns: a pathological withdrawal into an inner world and a desperate effort to evade society by flight. Critics and literary historians singled out the more obvious instances: the list included Poe, Hawthorne, Emily Dickinson, even Thoreau as victims of isolation; Henry James, Bret Harte, Stephen Crane, Lafcadio Hearn as exiles; Melville and Bierce simply as casualties of the environment. From this evidence maladjustment was assumed to be the normal fate of the American writer. Although Emerson, Whitman, and Mark Twain can hardly be considered to have been estranged from the national life in any practical sense, the critics of the 'twenties detected in their work the crippling effects of environment. For Brooks those effects appeared in the quality of Emerson's intellect: "The truth is that Emerson was imperfectly interested in human life; he cared little for experience or emotion, possessing so little himself."[4] This judgment was reiterated by Parrington, who found in Emerson "a certain starved and abstract quality, a lack of rich paganism that endows life and art with sensuous beauty";[5] and by Ludwig Lewisohn: "a mind that had no commerce with deep, primordial, tragic, human things, an almost abstract, disembodied mind, fine but thin, bloodless and so un-clouded, never somber, almost never troubled to its depth because it had no direct contact with the problems and conflicts ... which spring from human passions, rela-tions, longings, triumphs, desires."[6]

If Emerson's shortcoming for these critics was hyper-trophy of intellect, Whitman's and Mark Twain's was the reverse—a failure to arrive at intellectual maturity. Brooks wrote of Whitman: "Perfectly right in all his instincts, perfectly right so long as he kept to the plane of instincts, he was lost on the plane of ideas. . . . He had no ideas, and he was satisfied to have none. He lacked, above all, intensity. He was too complacent. He was incapable of discipline, and he did not see that discipline is, for Americans, the condition of all forward move-ment."[7] Parrington also comments on Whitman's and Mark Twain's immaturity. He writes of Whitman, "A great figure, the greatest assuredly in our literature—yet perhaps only a great child";[8] and of Twain, "All of his life he remained a boy, with the imitativeness of youth, and yet with something deep within him that cherished its own integrity."[9]

Brooks's gifts as biographer and student of culture were at their height in *The Ordeal of Mark Twain*, a demonstration of the tragic miscarriage of literary genius induced by the adverse pressures of family and environ-ment. The controversy precipitated by this work has not been settled; there is no unanimity of opinion about Brooks's judgment of Mark Twain's writing or of Mark Twain's environment. But it is clear that Brooks was applying far too rigorously a formula that is accepted in its general implications—the inevitable influence of en-vironment upon the work of art—and that he minimized the resources of conscious design available to the artist even when, like Mark Twain, he acquiesces in the con-straints of a culture. The point is that Mark Twain willed to be a representative writer and succeeded by sub-mitting to the ethos of his time and place.

11

In the 'twenties a different verdict might have been expected on those contemporaries who, heeding the liberal critics' admonitions, resisted the coercion of environment and employed realistic techniques to expose its faults. But apparently even when the writer, unlike his nineteenth-century predecessors, stood his ground and grappled with the actualities of American society he was not spared from the corrosive effect of his culture—the arresting in mid-career of his power and promise. The strictures of Brooks's *Letters and Leadership* are echoed in Lewisohn's reference to "the crucial and strange tragedy of the creative artist in America—his almost if happily not quite universal inability to develop—to strike within himself new rocks whence might spring living waters, his apparent petrifaction at a certain point. Dreiser has never developed beyond *Sister Carrie* nor Masters beyond *Spoon River,* nor Lewis beyond *Arrowsmith.*"[10]

A conviction of decadence disturbed the liberal criticism of the 'twenties. T. K. Whipple's *Spokesmen* (1928), for example, despite the sympathy and good will bestowed upon its subjects—Robinson, Dreiser, Frost, Anderson, Cather, Sandburg, Lindsay, Lewis, O'Neill— leaves the impression of an underlying pessimism far more convincing than the writer's contrary protestations. Almost without exception these writers are treated clinically—exhibits of the withering effects of American life. Robinson's "aloofness and reticence are results of his instinctive withdrawal from life, of his inability to make healthy, normal, fruitful contacts with his environment."

> Dreiser has assembled super-abundant material for a penetrating and radical criticism of American life. Yet as a thinker, as social critic, he has been rendered all but impotent by the influence of his environment. . . . More than most men, he has suffered from the absence of an established national literary tradition, with its attendant discipline in taste and critical standards.[11]

12

Among contemporary writers, Frost has been singularly fortunate in having found, for his incomplete but considerable capacity for experience, an environment which has yielded an experience not wholly inadequate.[12]

Anderson's performance suffers from the sort of stuff he has had to deal with. Compared with the imaginative worlds of the major British or French novelists, of Fielding or Balzac, say, the world of his making is a little poor, in the sense that it lacks variety, body, massiveness . . . but the responsibility rests not with Anderson, who has done the best he could, but with his environment.[13]

Her triumph over Nebraska implies that Miss Cather has also conquered the Nebraska in herself. . . . She has been able to go ahead and do the best of which she was capable—an achievement so rare in American literature as to verge on the miraculous.[14]

No doubt [Sandburg's] work suffers both in material and in form from the peculiarities of his environment.[15]

In short, [Sinclair Lewis] has not escaped contamination, but has partially conformed to his environment. One of the Lewises is a philistine.[16]

If O'Neill's dramatic world is narrow and meager, his characterization incomplete, if his imagination is not hale and robust, it is because that imagination, feeding upon a devitalized life inimical to human values, has suffered from undernourishment.[17]

Whipple's response to contemporary writing illustrates how devastating the application of Brooks's doctrine had become in the 1920's. Whipple's later development as a critic paralleled his master's: the essays written in the following decade (*Study Out the Land*) were affirmative about the native culture, but the affirmation was gained at the expense of denying aesthetic values and overvaluing the popular elements in culture for their own sake.

Works of the imagination, however indispensable to the study of a culture, do not constitute its most unequivocal documents, particularly when they are used to demonstrate its intellectual and moral constituents. They impose a further difficulty by adding an extra dimension—the aesthetic—to cultural investigation. A work like *The Education of Henry Adams* may serve the historically or psychologically minded critic better than, say, the novels of Henry James. Adams, for example, provides the principal theme of Whipple's *Spokesmen:*

> It is no wonder that Henry Adams drew the obvious moral: life is meaningless, a senseless tragedy of futility and waste. To arrive at this conclusion, he needed no knowledge of science or history: he needed only to observe himself and his world. That is the importance of Henry Adams—that he recorded the experience of a man endowed with the poetic temper and forced to live in a practical society, that he first and most fully formulated the philosophy implicit in American behavior, and that he therefore affords the best of all approaches to an understanding of modern American life and literature.[18]

The experience of James does not bear out the argument that pessimism is a correlative of environmental impediments to the poetic temper. For James the artist's vocation had a positive value; it remained an "ever fixèd mark" in a universe of flux and confusion. James, after all, managed to solve the problem of orientation in the modern world even if it involved residence in a "rented house." But if Adams does not perfectly epitomize the situation of the American artist, as Whipple implies, he is a crucial example of the effect of modern American culture upon the sensitive mind.

Among the ironies of Adams's sense of isolation, arising from his belief that there were not a half-dozen men in the United States capable of sharing his distress, is the fact that the *Education* became virtually a handbook for a whole generation. He suffered, of course, from an alienation far more impressive than a mere quarrel with his native culture. Neither Europe, nor the South Seas, nor art provided a resting place for this wanderer, because fundamentally he was an alien in his age and perceived no promise in any future development of human culture. The doctrine of the *Education* has sometimes been received with skepticism as well as with enthusiasm. The skeptics discount the philosophic basis of Adams's pessimism; in their view his picture of a declining civilization was merely an attempt to rationalize a personal sense of failure and frustration by endowing it with cosmic meanings. His stature as an artist and thinker, however, concerns us less than the relevance of his most influential work to the temper and thought of a generation preoccupied with ideas and images of dissolution.

The doctrine of *The Education of Henry Adams* is the ruin of the world, the running down of culture, and the desiccation of the sources of renewal in modern life. Adams's awareness of the modern dislocation propelled his constant search for a principle of unity, a law of history that would confer order upon chaos. Though the time was not ripe for religious conversion, his search for authority foreshadows the widespread reaction from liberal individualism later in the century. His representation of the "mediaeval synthesis" as the summit of human development was to be adopted by the later critics of modern culture.

Adams's social views, particularly his reservations about equalitarianism, were not palatable, however, to most American critics, though they shared his revulsion from the mercantile democracy that emerged after the Civil War. His sense of aristocratic isolation separated him also from Marx, to whose historical doctrine he had been drawn. Adams did, however, anticipate an important motive in the writings of the literary radicals—the censure of puritanism upon which their program for the liberation of American culture was founded. The puritan inheritance was no doubt too deeply ingrained in Adams to permit a tangible revolt on his part; but he clearly perceived the limitations that this powerful strain in the native culture had imposed upon his personality and upon the art of his American contemporaries. An essential difference between twelfth-century Europe and twentieth-century America noted by Adams was the suppression, in the latter, of the spontaneous sex energy.

Adams was far from indifferent to the aesthetic point of view; he valued art and religion as the supreme products of civilization. But his interests were mainly political, moral, and theological rather than literary. It was as moralist and social critic that he deeply impressed the critics for whom morals and society were in the forefront of the problem of American writing. They were probably more impressed by the moral atmosphere of *The Education*—its negativism, passivity, and desperation—than by its specific ideas. Quite apart from political or religious adherence, the contemporary intellectual recognized there the stamp of authenticity. "In its spiritual bafflements, its peculiarly native mixture of materialism and religious feeling, the desperate search for some central tradition [the] *Education* reads like a diary of our speculative conscience."[19]

It is not uncommon for one generation to disparage the pessimism of the age preceding. In retrospect, the pessimism of the 'twenties does seem self-indulgent, over-dramatized, perhaps exhibitionistic. Never a mass phenomenon, it was confined to an intellectual group, composed chiefly of artists and those concerned with the arts—men highly conscious of their distaste for the surface activities and the temper of the national life, which was, if anything, more self-satisfied and more energetic than ever before. Their pessimism has been characterized as unnecessarily misanthropic and anarchistic, unrelated to a philosophic center, too dependent upon personal frustration to represent a mature and tragic view. Never-

16

theless it cannot, as some have wished, be dismissed simply as a transitory literary fashion, nor as an aping of the world-weariness of European thought.

Disillusion and cynicism, products of war, were nourished by the insensate materialism and philistinism of the postwar years. The effect of naturalism, a literary movement that had gathered momentum ever since the beginning of the century, should not be underestimated either. Naturalism deflated the buoyant individualism of the nineteenth century by representing man as subject to overwhelming nonhuman forces—biological, physical, and economic. The determinist phase of literary naturalism was by no means uniformly pessimistic, nor was it employed as a consistent philosophic system; a Nietszchean titanism is evident in the novels of Jack London and Dreiser. But on the whole the naturalist novel encouraged pessimism, whereas its social description corroborated the censure of modern American life that lay at the center of literary radicalism.

Henry Adams diagnosed his failure in education as a failure to bridge the gap between the static, finite, agrarian-mercantile patriciate of the eighteenth century and the dynamic world of finance capitalism and industrial technology. This is an accurate description of the social discontent of the liberal critics. The most spectacular expression of the liberal attitude in the immediate postwar period was Harold Stearns's *Civilization in the United States,* a symposium designed to show "that the most moving and pathetic fact in the social life of America today is emotional and aesthetic starvation. . . . We have no heritages or traditions to which to cling except those that have already withered in our hands and turned to dust. One can feel the whole industrial and economic situation as so maladjusted to the primary and simple needs of men and women that the futility of a rationalistic attack on these infantilisms of compensation becomes obvious."[20] In the literary section of this survey Van Wyck Brooks reiterated the basic tenet of his

17

earlier tracts—that the coercive tyranny of a mechanized and centralized economy was choking off the potential outlets for the development of personality. The animus formerly directed against American civilization as a whole was here concentrated upon our "business civilization." Whereas Brooks's contribution was tinged with the pessimism common to the survey as a whole, Lewis Mumford's "The City" outlined the conception of an integrated culture based on the organic community which was to inform his major work in the two following decades. Mumford's emphasis was prophetic in that it subordinated economic and political questions to the totality of culture. His description of the early New England village as an organic community forecast the rediscovery of an authentic cultural tradition in the New England renaissance of the 1840's and 1850's. The affirmative sociology of Mumford was to influence Brooks's later development as a critic.

Insofar as literary criticism verges on social criticism in the present century, it has exhibited a fairly uniform and consistent revulsion from the moral and cultural attributes of industrialism: a materialistic and acquisitive ethics indifferent to human values; the glorification of mechanism and technology as opposed to vitality and spontaneity; the pressures making for a dead level of standardization and social conformity; mass production of popular literature and the arts; factitious cultural standards based on "the pillage of the past" together with ignorance of an indigenous artistic tradition.

Obviously industrialism alone did not account for the cultural sterility of which the postwar critics were convinced; European cultures had continued to flourish in an even more advanced stage of industrialization. The peculiar vulnerability of American culture was attributed to both the absence of an established native tradition and to the persistence of colonial timidity in cultural matters. The effects of industrialism were further abetted by two indigenous elements: puritan morality, the most

18

nearly permanent single tradition in American culture; and pioneer mentality, which eventually permeated the country, even the settled East. According to Waldo Frank, who made the most of this thesis, the pioneer and puritan strains were not separate entities, but actually identical, the former being a secularized and cruder version of the latter. Animosity toward industrial capitalism and the whole complex included under the name of puritanism—the attenuated culture of upper-class society dominated by academic and provincial standards; the judgment of art by exclusively moral standards; above all, prudery in literature—were staples of literary criticism of the 'twenties. Western critics naturally rejected attribution of the utilitarianism and vulgarity of American culture to the pioneer element; they wished to accredit the frontier with virtually all the genuine and vital elements in the national culture.

Aside from this regionalist dispute, the proponents of critical realism agreed upon two requirements for a flourishing literature: the artist's right to unhampered individual expression, and the necessity for unmasking the iniquities and stupidity of the existing social order. More than ever before, liberation and revolt were viewed as literary norms; the writer's quarrel with society was regarded as substantive in literary work. Given such sanction, the revolt against prevailing mores was sometimes fairly diffuse; political motives were often subsumed in personal ones. A journal like the *Masses-Liberator* advocated a socialist political program and a liberation aesthetics without reconciling the two. The antipuritan rebellion was joined by both the bohemian-aesthetic movement and the movement of critical realism. The impulse to rejection, once released, assimilated all dissidence indiscriminately. Originally directed against middle-class culture and mores, the movement embraced attacks on religion, on capitalism, on nationalism, on the national mythology, in short any resistance to the national life and ideas.

The doctrines of the literary radicals were seriously disputed only by the new humanists. Although they themselves were repelled by industrialism and by the anarchic tendencies of democratic society, the humanists had no sympathy for iconoclastic protests. Instead, they advocated return to the positive ethical values of Western culture that had survived in the puritan tradition. In the liberal-humanist controversy, sometimes regarded as the crucial literary event of the 1920's, liberalism had an unequal advantage in numbers if not in argument. Humanism, because of the restricted outlook of its leading figures, Irving Babbitt and Paul Elmer More, failed to survive as a permanent force in American criticism. The new humanists' aristocratic leanings eventually alienated critics who, like Stuart Sherman, admired the equalitarian and libertarian elements of the native political tradition; their indifference to contemporary experience and their inconclusive theology alienated T. S. Eliot, who shared their social and ethical views; their preoccupation with the ideological element in literature and their censoriousness toward the poetic imagination alienated a traditionalist and classicist like Allen Tate.

H. L. Mencken, the most vociferous opponent of the new humanism in the 'twenties, is too idiosyncratic to be listed with the liberals. Though his main interests were not literary, he found a wider audience than any other critic in the period. Yet his influence was short-lived; his criticism, improvisatory in nature, lacked a positive doctrinal center. His method was that of exposure and attack; it drew upon the prevailing attitudes of rejection that had been propagated by the liberal critics. His politics were as conservative and antiequalitarian as those of the new humanists, but his enthusiasm for all writing that dissected American manners and morals led him to defend the cause of critical realism.

Mencken's attack on puritanism and gentility sometimes appears to be argued on aesthetic grounds.

20

> The American . . . casts up all ponderable values, including even the values of beauty, in terms of right and wrong. . . . Naturally enough this moral obsession has given a strong color to American literature. In truth it has colored it so brilliantly that American literature is set off sharply from all other literatures. In none other will you find so wholesale and ecstatic a sacrifice of aesthetic ideas, of all the fine gusto of passion and beauty to the notion of what is meet, proper and nice.[21]

Despite Mencken's debt to the Continental aestheticism of the 'nineties, which had been conveyed to America by Huneker and others, he cannot be counted among the aesthetically oriented or formalist critics. Mencken's plea for aesthetic liberation was only incidental to his assault upon a specific sort of moral evaluation of literature. Both he and the liberal critics were pleading, not for a conception of art that transcends morality, but for a broader conception of morality in art.

A more single-minded exponent than Mencken of the view that American literature had been warped by puritanism was Ludwig Lewisohn. In a period when most critics, liberal and reactionary alike, were discarding the nineteenth-century ideal of unregenerate individualism, Lewisohn insisted on the artist's innate privilege of self-expression. "In the modern poet, as in the bard, experience and expression are one. But his experience is not tribal; it is wholly individual; it tends . . . to have, as one important element, a revolt from the tribal."[22] Not only did Lewisohn reject the "formalist" conception of the artist as craftsman, in the derisive term "artificer," but he quarreled with the leading notion of the other liberal critics that art and society are inextricably linked.

> In the study and interpretation of the arts we can dismiss in respect of the individual's possibility of expression and his special approach to it, the pressure of environment. Every age and land is the right age and land for creative expression. . . . Hence the

21

genesis of art, of all inevitable expression, is in the poet's soul; age, country, fortune, do but determine method and convention—the common denominator of all communication.[23]

From this it follows that the artist must surmount the shortcomings of his environment and achieve art by asserting his own deviation from the norms of his time and place. "The true history of literature in America is the history of those poets and thinkers who first in mere theory, later in both theory and practice, denied the Puritan division of experience from expression."[24]

Lewisohn's dismissal of the determinist notion is not actually borne out in his studies of particular authors. Although he located the springs of artistic expression in the psyche, he was no less concerned than any of the other liberal critics with demonstrating the deleterious effects of the American environment upon the psyche. Lewisohn was among the first critics in America to apply the psychoanalytic doctrine to literature, and the only critic to base upon it a literary history. The Freudian conception of personality was highly illuminating to those who attributed the failure of American literature to personal frustration and unfulfillment. They were primarily concerned not with Freud's method but with his "subversive" philosophy, posited on the conflict between man's instincts and social conventions. Lewisohn employed the theory to protest against artificial barriers to self-expression as well as to rationalize his own conviction that the sexual repressions implicit in American culture had either inhibited or distorted the American writer's capacity for expression.

The negativism of critics during the 'twenties in discussing American culture makes credible the unified *Zeitgeist* to which Van Wyck Brooks referred in his recantation. It will be recalled that in his earliest writings the rebellious spirit appeared as a prime desideratum of literature; throughout the decade the creative impulse itself was identified with nonconformity. The idea of

22

dissidence as a condition of literary excellence did not, however, originate in a single conception of literature. One of its phases was a corollary of the writer's right to self-expression and to free experiment—the notion of the artist's special privilege in a society dominated by a bourgeois laity. Another phase was primarily concerned, not with the writer's autonomy, but with the social utility of literature. Lewisohn and Mencken took the former position; Brooks and the sociological critics, the latter. The preëminent exemplar of the sociological method was Vernon L. Parrington, of whom Alfred Kazin has written:

> It was rebelliousness as a principle that carried Parrington through his work. He was a rebel and a friend to all rebels; he exulted in any aggressive liberalism to a point where he found more crusaders in American life than perhaps ever existed and certainly more rebellion in his worthies than some of them ever displayed. . . . He identified rebellion with the creative impulse, and that impulse with America.[25]

By 1930 the unity of the *Zeitgeist* was no longer apparent; liberal criticism—an ambiguous designation for various dissident tendencies—had undergone a gradual transformation, which was now revealed as an urgent need to resolve its uncertainties. The limits of denunciation having been reached, the inevitable occurred: a period of affirmation began to take shape. By this time the attack on American civilization had shifted its sights from the total environment, material and intellectual, to the "business civilization"; one could now reclaim the moral and intellectual legacy of the American past as the basis for a positive tradition without renouncing liberal principles. The cultural nationalism of Van Wyck Brooks is one of the metamorphoses of liberal criticism; it was an emotional rather than a doctrinal conversion, since he had from the beginning affirmed the national basis of art.

The conversion from liberal dissidence to Marxism, no less emotional, was another phase of the will to affirma-

23

tion. Marxism was able to assimilate and absorb the rebellious tendencies of liberal criticism by sublimation; revolt was to be collectivized by purging it of individualistic content and harnessing its energy to a mass movement. The revolutionary argument was fortified by appeals to the record of dissent in the national letters; an effort was made to establish it as the sole authentic American tradition. Parrington's *Main Currents in American Thought* was absorbed, with some reservations, into the Marxist literary canon along with much of the contemporary social fiction that had been defended by the liberal critics. The Marxists were willing to receive the devastating account of contemporary life rendered by the alienated sensibility, if they could impose upon it their own meaning. Thus (according to Granville Hicks, at one time the leading critic of the movement) Dreiser, Lewis, and Anderson failed to achieve order, form, and significance in their work because they failed to perceive these qualities in their environment. The chaos of American life that overwhelmed the critical realists was, according to this view, merely an illusion; given the instrument of political analysis, the chaos is perceived to be a unified, orderly phenomenon of class conflicts.[26] The emotional appeal of Marxism to critics, however, had little to do with its literary methods or values, but lay in its prediction of a society where chaos would be replaced by order, skepticism by faith, disintegration by unity—a society, in other words, that released the individual from the burden of alienation so conspicuous in American letters.

Nearly all critics who have been concerned with the question of alienation in American writing assume a fairly direct connection between literature and environment. They are usually at their best, therefore, when discussing works in which environment is an explicit element. But if the connection is devious or obscure, as in the writings of Henry James, the formula itself be-

24

comes problematical. During the past half century the case of Henry James has become labyrinthine, not unlike a great legal controversy involving treason which arouses men's most passionate prejudices and convictions. His career drew attention to the status of the literary profession in the United States; the extraordinary method and matter of his works compelled attention to the relation between literature and culture. It was almost impossible for American critics to remain neutral or merely indifferent to James.

In the first years of this century, critics were preoccupied with the plain fact of James's repudiation of the United States as a place of residence; they failed to consider the ambivalence and subtlety of his relation to his country—his own awareness of what was lost and what was gained by expatriation. A sense of outrage at James's disloyalty, coupled with a distaste for the involutions of his prose, made it difficult for some critics to view his work without violent prejudice. The point of view of Herbert Croly,[27] though not extravagant, was highly atypical. Croly dismisses James's expatriation as irrelevant to the quality of his works, which, as the product of a highly individual talent, were to be judged on their own merit. James's reputation in the United States, which had been at its lowest ebb during his lifetime, improved after his death (in 1916) and has continued to rise. Today he ranks among the monumental figures of the nineteenth century. As criticism of James proliferated, resentment with his expatriation receded, but nearly all his critics have perceived that James's personal relation to American culture and American society has an essential bearing on the content and the quality of his fiction. T. S. Eliot was among the first to point out the continuity of James's work in the native American tradition as well as its essentially national flavor.

One trend in recent James criticism has been to counterbalance the conventional estimate by minimizing his estrangement from America and vindicating the native element in his work. Although his alienation was ambivalent, alternating (as his correspondence reveals) between extremes of attraction and repulsion, it was a constant and conscious element in both his personality and his work. But only as it acts upon his work is it the critic's legitimate concern. For the liberal critics, James was the prime specimen of the writer whose gifts had been vitiated by expatriation. For Brooks, Parrington, and Matthew Josephson, James was an incarnation of failure, of isolation from American experience, of flight from the artist's responsibilities. The rejection of James sometimes assumed an almost hysterical quality. According to Waldo Frank, "He was a strange sort of monster . . . with vast peripheral development and no depths. . . . All his life he gave up to the creation of a world rootless like himself, brilliant and intricate and superficial like his own centrifugal life."[28] Parrington's "excommunication" of James from the national literary roster has by now become something of a scandal.

Aversion to Henry James, still fairly widespread, is explicable in those who wish, in the words of F. W. Dupee, "to keep our literary image comparatively simple, comparatively faithful to our democratic professions."[29] His repudiation by critics who have been particularly sensitive to the problems of the alienated American writer is more difficult to assess. James himself was extraordinarily aware of the burdens laid on the American artist, not the least of which was the prospect of atrophy and truncation. His ironic diagnosis of the artist's plight in an early story prefigures the mood of the 'twenties.

> We're the disinherited of art! We're condemned to be superficial! We're excluded from the magic circle! The soil of American perception is a poor little barren artificial deposit! We're wedded to imperfection! An American to excel, has just ten times as much to learn as a European! We lack the deeper sense! We have neither tact nor force! How

should we have them? Our crude and garish climate, our silent past, our deafening present.... We poor aspirants must live in perpetual exile.[30]

Since the young Henry James was no more inclined to resignation than the young Van Wyck Brooks, the narrator in this story speaks, as F. O. Matthiessen points out, for James's hopes: "Nothing is so idle as to talk about our want of a nursing air, of a kindly soil, of opportunity, of the things that help. The only thing that helps is to do something fine. There's no law in our glorious Constitution against that. Invent, create, achieve."

Of course James, contrary to the normal experience in American letters, did not stagnate, but persevered in expanding the possibilities of his craft. One would think that this fact—quite apart from the merit of his last works—might have illuminated the intricate relation between the writer and society. The liberal critics, however, questioned the validity of any writing that did not directly expose the evils of industrial democracy. They were entitled to their antipathy for James's mature works certainly, but they justified their exasperation on mistaken grounds. They charged that James became a romantic, evading reality in a solipsistic version of life; that his preoccupation with form eventually preëmpted the writer's reliance on experience. Their a priori notion of realism, confined to social realism of the naturalist variety, kept them from perceiving James's devotion to the realistic principle. His vision of reality was refracted through an extraordinary sensibility and further transformed by the demands of his conception of the art of fiction. Still, as R. P. Blackmur has said, it remained authentic.

On the level of the ideal—on the level of art— American fiction achieved in the novels and short stories of Henry James a kind of reality different from both the literal record of a Howells and the philosophic naturalism of a Zola. This reality was his response to the human predicament of his gen-

27

eration. . . . With his abiding sense of the inde-
structible life, he expressed the decay and sterility of
a society pretending to live on convention and
institutions but lacking the force of underlying convictions. He described what he saw, and created
what lay under what he saw.[31]

James's insight into the American writer's handicap is
based upon knowledge of the formative role of culture
in literary work. This insight is not only a recurrent theme
in his fiction, but the subject of his essay on Hawthorne.
"The flower of art blooms only where the soil is deep. . . .
It needs a complex social machinery to set a writer in
motion. American civilization has hitherto had other
things to do than to produce flowers, and before giving
birth to writers, it has wisely occupied itself with providing something for them to write about."[32] The essay
anticipates two of the important strictures that critics in
the following century were to make concerning the
United States as a setting for artists and art. First, James
perceives the damaging effect of the puritan ethos on
the life of realization—a staple of the American critical
outlook in the 1920's.

American life had begun to constitute itself from
the foundations; it had begun to *be,* simply; it was
at an immeasurable distance from having begun to
enjoy. I imagine there was no appreciable group of
people in New England at that time proposing to
enjoy life. . . . I say that [Hawthorne] must have
proposed to himself to enjoy, simply because he
proposed to be an artist, and because this enters
inevitably into the artist's scheme. . . . He proposes
to give pleasure, and to give it he must first get it.
Where he gets it will depend on circumstances, and
circumstances were not encouraging to Hawthorne.[33]

Then, James notes the absence in America of a self-
conscious intellectual class, and the consequence for the
writer.

Fifty years ago, greatly more than now, the literary

28

man must have lacked the comfort and inspiration of belonging to a class. The best things come, as a general thing, from the talents that are members of a group; every man works better when he has companions working in the same line, and yielding to the stimulus of suggestion, comparison, emulation. Great things of course have been done by solitary workers; but they have usually been done with double the pains they would have cost if they had been produced in more genial circumstances.[34]

The implications of these remarks exceed the example of Hawthorne in that they are both personal and general: they illuminate James's own designs, and they describe a common situation. James's diagnosis did not lead him to conclusions about the artist's inevitable doom in America. As a critic he takes full account of the social ingredients in literature but avoids inferring the nature of the literary work from the writer's environment. James's notions of literary causation were derived, not from a philosophic or historic rationale, but from his own experience as a creative artist. The literary theories of liberal critics, on the other hand, often ignored the actual process of literary composition; they apparently assumed the direct conversion of social and personal experience into literary products.

Henry James implied that the American writer's opportunity to associate with an artistic or intellectual elite had improved since Hawthorne's time; but the critics of the 'twenties would have considered this view unduly sanguine. The artist's isolation in America—his inevitable severance from collective life—was one of their prime tenets. Nearly a hundred years earlier Tocqueville had predicted the atomization of a society based on democratic individualism. "Thus not only does democracy make every man forget his ancestors, but it hides his descendants, and separates his contemporaries from him; it throws him back forever upon himself alone, and threatens in the end to confine him entirely within the solitude of his own heart." The stock image of the American artist in the 'twenties was that of the exile, the fugitive from society, who ends up either eccentric or morbid. In the criticism of this period Hawthorne's imagination appears in a light far removed from the relatively benign account of Henry James. Hawthorne's name is often linked with Poe's to illustrate the psychoneurotic results of deliberate aloofness from social realities. There has since been a movement to qualify or to refute the conception of Hawthorne as an aberrant; but in Matthew Josephson's *Portrait of the Artist as an American,* which summarizes the leading ideas of the liberal critics, the preoccupations of Poe and Hawthorne are taken to represent a constant element: "In a large measure the strain of morbidity in Hawthorne and Poe seems to have been handed on. The obsession with evil, early sorrow, and death appears astonishingly native to the American muse."[35]

A preoccupation with horror and violence far more deeply imagined and far more compelling than the conventions of Gothic romance has indeed persisted in American writing—a phenomenon often more evident to Europeans than to ourselves. D. H. Lawrence, for example, concluded that decadence must be endemic in our literature; though American writers imagined they acquired it from Europe, they were really reimporting their own product. Lawrence attributed American decadence to a quasi-mystical origin, the white man's inability to come to terms with the physical environment of the New World.

> As I say, it is perhaps easier to love America passionately, when you look at it through the wrong end of the telescope, across the Atlantic water, as Cooper did so often, than when you are right there. When you are actually *in* America, America hurts, because it has a powerful disintegrative influence

upon the white psyche. . . . America is tense with latent violence and resistance.[36]

The liberal critics, and subsequently the Marxists, some of whom had been disciples of Van Wyck Brooks, had more rational explanations for the decadent strain in American writing, which had become even more pronounced during the first three decades of the twentieth century; they ascribed it to the singularities of American social environment and intellectual culture. According to Newton Arvin, the efflorescence of decay in contemporary American writing was the tragic price paid for the hypertrophy of social, political, and philosophic individualism.

> For the story of American letters is the story of the blossoming, the fruition, and the corruption of exactly the individualism that is now on trial. . . . In [Emerson, Thoreau, Whitman] our individualism, on its brighter side, attained its classic meridian. There was of course, even then, a darker side . . . confusion, morbidity, and a kind of impotence . . . and Poe, Hawthorne, and Melville, men of the richest endowments, paid a tragic price for sitting on pumpkins and effusing egotism. . . . By the second decade of the century we found ourselves in the midst of an individualistic revolt which superficially seemed to appeal to the authority of Emerson, Thoreau, and Whitman, but which, unlike theirs, was radically personal and antisocial. It had been anticipated, a few years before, by the Nietzschean egoism of Jack London and the antinomianism of Dreiser; and it was to mingle the elements of misanthropy, transcendentalism, anarchism, and high aspiration in bewildering proportions. The new individualism ran the gamut from the Menckenian-Cabellian praise of aristocracy to Anderson's primitivism and O'Neill's romantic affirmations, from Lewis's exposure of the standardized bourgeois to V. W. Brooks subtle studies in frustration.[37]

31

As has been observed in the discussion of Henry James, it is easier to demonstrate alienation in the writer's personality than to deduce its palpable effects on his work. For strategic purposes, however, the liberal critics, and later the Marxists, equated alienation and decadence. This confusion was ably exposed by James T. Farrell, who rejects the polarization of growth and decay as categories of literary judgment and the ascription of the label "decadent" to every work whose subject matter is disintegration.[38] We must guard against the facile coupling of the writer's environment and his art which at the same time ignores the ways in which his relation to his culture illuminates his work. The writer's alienation from society may sometimes induce a morbid engrossment in his own infirmities, but it may also, as with Henry James, lead to suppression of the subjective element and a compensatory emphasis on the objectivity of art. Both topics—the psychology of alienation in writers and aestheticism as an outlet for alienation—have been treated exhaustively by contemporary critics.

The psychology of alienation is most patent in writers who, capitalizing upon their differentiation from the social norm, have projected their visions of reality in terms of their private maladjustments. The subject had surpassing interest for sociological critics, particularly if they were imbued with the idea of literature as a medium of social reform. But in the hands of the liberal and Marxist critics, it was sometimes exploited for an indiscriminate attack upon contemporary literature.

> Like tortured introverts, contemporary writers have turned in every direction in an endeavor to discover new reservoirs of impulse within themselves, explored every emotion in an attempt to find new strength, exploit every idea in a desperate hope of creating a new ideal. Lost in the pathological loneliness of individual identity detached from the social strength of the group they have battered against the walls of personality, bludgeoned their way into the

catacombs of the unconscious, and with maniacal determination released in the instinctual energies of primeval man which still live within the human frame.[39]

Alienation in modern writing was most strenuously censured by the Marxist critics, whose program was therapeutic: the writer's participation in society by way of revolutionary politics was proposed as a cure. But even in times of social fervor, the artist does not willingly relinquish the prerogative of individuality. Consequently, a minority of critics has always been prepared to vindicate the modern writer's alienation on psychological and historical grounds. In recent years this position has been most eloquently upheld by those whose disillusion with Marxism has been proportionate to their former enthusiasm.

The title essay of Edmund Wilson's *The Wound and the Bow* (1941) precipitated a fresh discussion of the role of alienation in modern writing. A decade earlier, in *Axel's Castle,* Wilson had described the tremendous expansion in sensibility and technique achieved by the heirs of symbolism. His tribute to these writers is qualified, however, by his conclusion: there, renouncing that point of view in literature which presses the individual's case at the expense of the social whole, Wilson urges the writer to participate in man's social adventure. Although his later criticism does not abandon the social and historical perspective, it shifts the stress from environmental pressures to the formative influence of individual psychology in a writer's work. "The Wound and the Bow" adumbrates a theory that connects literary genius with the pathology of the writer. The theme of the essay is that the trauma experienced by a writer may become the source of his literary power; but, as Lionel Trilling has noted, it is not entirely clear whether Wilson intended to postulate a general causal connection between neurosis and literary genius.

The juxtaposition of art and neurosis suggested by

33

Wilson was more fully explored by a group associated with *Partisan Review,* notably William Phillips, William Barrett, and Philip Rahv, whose views were developed during a period of acute political and moral disillusionment—the Second World War. Whereas the liberals of the 'twenties had repudiated the elements of disintegration in contemporary writing and supported only its rebelliousness, the "insurgent" critics of the 'forties constructed a rationale of alienation by certifying the authenticity of those elements. To confirm it, they adduced the triumphs of the great exponents of anxiety and neurosis in modern literature—Dostoevski, Nietzsche, Baudelaire, Kafka, and Proust. Reviving the ancient notion that the poetic vocation is deranged per se, Barrett proposes that the writer's alienation is intrinsic.

> But why (in the end) should it be the writer's fate—more than of any other intellectual profession—to confront this crack in the face of the world? Because his subject is the very world of experience as such, and it is this world, this total world which he must somehow salvage. . . . Out of the ravages of his experience, his desperate loneliness, he must put forth those works which look back into his gaze with conviction and authenticity.[40]

Phillips does not insist that neurosis in literature has been universal, but he sees it as absolutely binding upon literary consciousness in the last century.

> Neurosis is not simply a spur to creative work but is deeply ingrained in it, and . . . the neurotic work somehow becomes the characteristic product of modern culture. . . . The critic cannot help but be . . . impressed by the fact that the conflicts, tensions, and neuroses of the literary man have become symptoms of the fate of culture in the West and are connected with at least one side . . . of the modern sensibility.[41]

Philip Rahv concurs in the belief that alienation in one form or another is the distinguishing feature of the litera-

ture of the modern world. For him the only significant
exception is Tolstoi, who evaded the disintegrating
effects of introspection and withdrawal by adhering to
an old-fashioned eighteenth-century rationalism founded
on the belief in a norm of human behavior. Thus Tolstoi's
best work displays neither the characteristic narcissism
of modern writing—manifested in hermetic withdrawal,
bohemian irresponsibility, eccentricity, and the loss of an
objective grip on the world of social reality—nor the
complementary preoccupation with the aesthetic, which
is one of the refuges of the alienated artist.

> [Tolstoi] has no interest in language as such, he is
> the enemy of rhetoric as such and every kind of
> artifice and virtuosity. The conception of writing as
> of something calculated and constructed—a con-
> ception first formulated explicitly by Edgar Allan
> Poe, upon which literary culture has become
> more and more dependent—is entirely foreign to
> Tolstoi. . . . For Tolstoi continually dissociated him-
> self from literature . . . as an autonomous way of life,
> a complete fate in the sense in which the French
> writers of Flaubert's generation conceived of it. . . .
> From the very first Tolstoi instinctively recognized
> the essential insufficiency and makeshift character
> of the narrowly aesthetic outlook, of the purely
> artistic appropriation of the world.[42]

In the United States, aestheticism—art for art's sake—
is often regarded as an exotic growth; yet there is an
indigenous aesthetic tradition in our letters reaching
back to Poe. It might have been even stronger except
for the native bias in favor of the moral and didactic
element in literature. The critic was generally suspicious
of the aesthetic, even when not actively hostile toward
it. For the liberal and Marxist critics, "aestheticism" and
"art for art's sake" were terms of severe opprobrium;
although "aesthetic" is by no means synonymous with
"aestheticism," it shared the latter's disrepute. But to
deprecate the aesthetic element in literature is to ignore

the difference between the writer's specific function and his general human or social nature. The antiaesthetic prejudice, furthermore, prevents a genuine historical understanding and fosters antipathy toward modern literature as such. In their zeal to bring about a milieu more favorable to the pursuit of the arts in America, the liberal and Marxist critics were often indifferent to the innate requirements of art. This insensitivity explains their incapacity for grasping imaginatively the problem of alienation in American writing, both past and present.

The aesthetic movement of the nineteenth century acquired its disrepute from a gratuitous desire to shock the bourgeois and from a social distemper that was hardly defensible, even though it had been provoked by philistinism. Whether or not bohemianism was foreign to the native temperament, its aesthetic outlook was widely accepted in Huneker's era. Huneker introduced into the American literary scene the atmosphere of *fin de siècle* but left no permanent impression upon literary thought. An omnivorous amateur of the arts, he had few positive aesthetic ideas. Mencken, the proponent of realism in fiction, admired Huneker for his iconoclasm toward American gentility; but most of the liberals censured his epicureanism, his predilection for "decadent" European art.

The aesthetic doctrine that flourishes in American criticism today owes little or nothing to the earlier aesthetic movement. Though international in its orientation, it has an unmistakably native accent. According to F. O. Matthiessen,

> This unusual degree of detachment which reverberates with loneliness, but which brings with it in compensation a special development of spiritual understanding, has grown organically out of the conditions of American life, out of the isolation of the individual from the centre of European culture. Kindred isolation enabled Thoreau and Emily Dickinson to study themselves with such rare mas-

tery. It also enabled Poe and Henry James and Eliot, all of them possessing the excessive provincial consciousness of elements in literary tradition which Europeans would have taken for granted—and ignored—by that very consciousness, to lead their European contemporaries into a more penetrating comprehension of the nature of art.[43]

The new criticism is neither bohemian nor irresponsible, but ascetic and consecrated. It is the first body of criticism in America possessing a philosophic groundwork and enough theoretical discipline to oppose the reigning assumptions of historical and sociological criticism.

The American genealogy of this criticism is complicated, reaching back in one direction (that of an uncompromising aesthetic standard) through J. E. Spingarn to Poe, and in another to the new humanism of Babbitt and More, whose standards were ethical and authoritarian. Its principles were crystallized by Ezra Pound and especially by T. S. Eliot, whose criticism, recapitulating the practice of Henry James, united aesthetic awareness with moral seriousness. (James's detachment from the literary scene may well have delayed the appearance of a mature criticism in the United States. In the long period when his creative and critical achievements were being ignored or misunderstood, he might have provided the corrective to the amateur and doctrinaire aspects of American criticism. Only in the past thirty years has there been a concerted effort to assimilate his work in a usable critical tradition.)

Nineteenth-century aestheticism, particularly the art-for-art's-sake movement, was closely allied with romantic doctrines of individual expression. By contemporary standards it was a spurious aestheticism, emphasizing the autonomy of the artist, not that of the work itself. The new criticism, on the other hand, has little sympathy with romantic art and less with romantic individualism. Its tastes are classical; it stresses discipline and craft, discrediting the use of art as a vehicle for personal utterance. It likewise discredits criticism that dwells on the writer's psychology as a genetic factor in literary composition. The proper object of criticism, according to this view, is the literary work perceived as an integral and autonomous whole—autonomous because it provides the reader with experience distinct in kind, not only from the writer's experience before its composition, but from all other experience. Strictly applied, aesthetic analysis rules out all extraliterary evidence, whether psychological or environmental; it requires the critic to concentrate on the formal elements constituting the uniqueness of the work. In order to defend a theory so alien to the prevailing intellectual mode, the new critics devoted considerable energy to exploding the main fallacy of contemporary criticism: specification of the communicative element as essential and of the formal element as supererogatory or ornamental. This tactic exposed them to the countercharge of superficial formalism. Actually their notion of form stipulates the integral connection of form and matter; the generic property of the aesthetic is the fusion of formal and nonformal elements. Hence they deny that a literary work can be judged by nonliterary criteria.

The reconstitution of criticism on an aesthetic basis is sometimes construed as a rationalization of indifference to all except literary values; its proponents, as Morton D. Zabel notes, were accused of defection from contemporary reality.

> The departure from American shores of Ezra Pound and T. S. Eliot was a hint that their talents were indifferent to the revival of an American ideal of the promotion of new standards of social realism. Their lodestone was neither the real nor the humanitarian; it was art.[44]

To what extent the doctrine of the new critics is a product of historic and psychological conditions, among which is the alienation of the modern writer, need not be argued here. But unquestionably the problem of alienation is relevant to their work. Their revulsion from contemporary American culture is unambiguous; it is linked with the fact that they are usually poets first and critics second. The cultural gap between modern verse and contemporary society, being greater than that between realistic fiction and American life, has reinforced their awareness of isolation.

Since the aesthetic principle proscribes the use of historical and psychological evidence to support literary judgment, the writer's alienation is irrelevant to the question of excellence, which depends only on the formal integrity of the work itself. Although these strictures delimit the scope of literary judgments, the proscription of historical method does not necessarily signify ignorance of history or social indifference. Contemporary aesthetic criticism operates within the framework of a positive social and cultural criticism that proceeds, not from the presumption that modern literature has failed, but from the perception that modern literature has been severed from the total culture. The idea of alienation (though not the term itself) is thus removed from the province of literary discourse and restored to its original historical and philosophical use. It becomes the central theme of an eccentric, yet highly impressive, world view in which the specific problem of the American writer is only subordinate.

2

Literature and Society: Two Versions

WE ARE OFTEN reminded that our period is remarkable
for the brilliance of its criticism. This view we are all the
more willing to corroborate now that we have abandoned
the old cyclical theory of creative and critical periods,
according to which a flourishing criticism signified the
diversion of artistic energy into discursive channels. The
final test of criticism is its efficacy as a medium or instrument for apprehending and evaluating literary works.
Contemporary criticism has been more successful in fulfilling this function than the designation "brilliant" sug-
gests. But although its main achievement is technical, its
peculiar quality derives from secondary attributes—the
very ones that confer upon criticism its importance as an
intellectual discipline.

The reigning intellectual mode is the method of
science, which prides itself upon transcending subjective
judgments—indeed, the whole realm of value. Criticism
has not always resisted the temptation to convert itself
into an objective science; but the effort has usually failed,
since value must remain the primary concern of criticism.
The peculiar importance of criticism today is explained
by the general defection of intellect from values, particularly those which apply to man's moral and spiritual
predicament. Not content to remain in its proper technical sphere—the elucidation and evaluation of literary
works—criticism now tends to appropriate areas normally reserved for philosophy, religion, and politics. The
nature of the literary medium seems to sanction such
excursions. Except when criticism has imposed upon
itself the severe limitations of induction, it has always
commented on morals. But never before our own time

40

has it essayed so ambitious a role—that of the intellectual "conscience" of an age.

This present role, extending the normal propensity of criticism to venture beyond its technical limits, has evoked protests against the dispersion of its interests. The chief issue today is the dispute between two approaches to literature: the extrinsic approach, by attempting to locate literature in the widest possible context of extraliterary conditions, enters the realm of historical, social, or philosophical values; the intrinsic approach, although denying the relevance of extraliterary information to the technical act of criticism, is not less concerned with these values, and the rationale of its method is derived from the larger framework of history, philosophy, and sociology.

That literature is intimately connected with the life of society was discovered rather late. Not until the nineteenth century was this insight formed into a full-fledged critical method. The historical critic attempted primarily to explain literary works as products of prevailing forces or currents in the writer's environment. The emphasis had shifted from style, technique, and the moral effects of literature to the exposition of origins. The more scientific the criticism, the less it emphasized the individual consciousness in the genesis of the work. The sociological method enjoyed a prodigious success; until rather recently it was dominant, particularly in American criticism. Of course even the most rigorous exponents of the sociological approach to literature, although insisting upon the priority of social determinants, are bound to consider the psychological ingredients in the genetic process; the most skillful historical critics of both the nineteenth and twentieth centuries perceived the complex relations between the creative consciousness and supraindividual determinants. The sociological and psychological methods are thus complementary rather than antithetical. But whether the critic assumes that the writer expresses the environment (the premise of the

41

sociological method) or that he is necessarily atypical (the premise of the psychological method), historical criticism concentrates on the relation, direct or indirect, between the literary work and its external circumstances.

Contemporary criticism owes much of its brilliance to the vast expansion of the historical method by psychology, linguistic science, and the social sciences. Sometimes, indeed, the proliferation of knowledge brought to bear upon literature has seemed to obscure the existence of the work itself. The historical method was at length assailed precisely because it threatened the integrity of the literary work. It was challenged by a philosophic conception of the literary work considered as art. Its opponents introduced or, more exactly, reintroduced into criticism the importance of the aesthetic property in literature, an idea that encountered stiff resistance since it had never become wholly naturalized. According to all nonaesthetic literary theories, a work is a phenomenon in a cultural continuum; to explain its nature and significance, one must analyze the elements in the environment that contributed to its origin or those that in turn are affected by the constituted work. The antihistorical critic designates these theories as the genetic and the affective fallacies respectively. Though he perceives that the work is a product of culture, subject to use by society, he maintains that criticism should treat it as a finite, discrete entity, discarding information about its origin and utility. In the logic of this exclusion, the aesthetic is conceived as the property that distinguishes the work of art from all other cultural objects—namely, its concrete particularity. Since the virtue of the aesthetic element is its autonomy—its discontinuity from other cultural phenomena and therefore from history—it cannot be enhanced by reference to conditions extrinsic to the work.

The premise of the ontological status of the literary work underlies the accomplishments of contemporary aesthetic criticism: concentration upon the actual text, and examination of internal features as parts of an integrated whole. Both the literary theory and the critical program of aesthetic criticism proscribe speculations of the sort ascribed to contemporary criticism in general. But the breach between the historical and the aesthetic approaches is less complete in practice than in theory. Historical critics have never actually dispensed with aesthetic criteria; without having made the principle of aesthetic judgment an integral part of their critical systems, they have usually paid it at least lip service. Even the most extreme relativists and determinists have not succeeded in exorcising from their work the habit of aesthetic pronouncements. The aesthetic critic, to be sure, specifies the aesthetic as the distinguishing property of literature; but only in rare instances would he regard aesthetic analysis as exhausting the function of criticism. It has been charged that the aesthetic critic, by ruling out the relevance of conditions anterior to composition, regards the work as existing in a historical vacuum. Yet it does not follow that he is ignorant of history or indifferent to morals or society. In subscribing to a belief in standards, whether aesthetic or moral, he must recognize their dependence upon the transmission of culture and hence upon the stability of society. The idea of aesthetic autonomy, itself the product of modern historical consciousness, presumes the knowledge of the nature of culture and social organization. On the rational level, the aesthetic critics preclude social and political views in their judgment of specific literary works; but much of their writings is devoted to nonliterary matters—mainly social and cultural questions. In this indirect way, then, aesthetic critics are just as much occupied with society as sociological critics.

Though the social and political views of contemporary critics are anything but unanimous, they issue from a single premise—a profound dissatisfaction with the fiber and quality of modern society. This revulsion is by no means peculiar to critics: it is an obsessive theme of modern imaginative literature and an engrossment of

43

modern thought. But the critic's vocation, which is ultimately judicial, conditions his social outlook; it coincides with neither that of the imaginative writer nor that of the sociologist. A sense of immanent cultural decline is the critic's mandate to investigate, not only the general relations between literature and society (the sociology of literature), but also the literary man's immediate relation to his society (politics).

The use of art as an index and measure of cultural achievement is fully sanctioned by students of culture. Professional sociologists and social philosophers like Spengler, Pareto, Sorokin, and Joad have evinced the decadence of modern art as one proof of the decline of culture as a whole. Unfortunately there are no generally accepted criteria of what constitutes decadence in art. On a very rudimentary level, it corresponds to a moral judgment passed upon subject matter that is repugnant to the individual. On another level, it often signifies no more than inertia in responding to new modes or styles or art—in other words, cultural lag. Because of temporal fluctuations of taste and moral conventions, it is not surprising that so many new masterpieces have been charged with decadence. The term "decadent" has lost all specific reference and has thus forfeited its technical usefulness in criticism. We lack an adjective to describe the characteristic literary product of a disintegrated culture, for which "romantic" is no longer adequate and "modernist" not explicit enough. Whatever the imperfections of such literary works, they do not correspond precisely to the imperfections of their milieu, for much contemporary literature is, by aesthetic standards, highly integrated.

The critic who subscribes to the doctrine of social determinism is logically bound, however, to infer the decadence of art from the decadence of society. ("The art of a decadent epoch 'must' be decadent; this is inevitable; and it would be futile to become indignant about it."[1])

44

Insofar as the dislocations of modern life and sensibility inhere in modern literature, there will be an inevitable correspondence—the primary one between art and reality—to support the sociological thesis. Because of the prevailing conviction of cultural decline, it seems legitimate to characterize modern literature as a literature of decadence. But the term "decadent literature" is not merely descriptive; it denotes a value judgment, moral or aesthetic. To use the attributive "decadent" is to identify literary quality with theme or subject matter; and behind this lies a more fundamental error, which reduces literary criteria to those of practical experience.

Since the sociological critic, like the cultural historian, is often concerned mainly with establishing the generic aspects of the volume of literature in an era, he is more disposed to regard modern literature as inevitably decadent than the critic who, believing that a work can be justly apprehended only as a finite aesthetic whole, examines and assesses it according to the internal evidence. One merit of the latter approach is its fidelity to the process of composition. To a creative artist in any period, the hypothesis that his work is predestined to be decadent in the ordinary sense is neither palatable nor even acceptable. Even if he knows the deficiencies of his culture, he is sustained by the conviction that his own powers are adequate to his immediate task. The aesthetic critic avoids blanket condemnations of the art of an era. But to grant that excellent art is being produced in a disintegrating or decadent culture is not equivalent to stipulating the total insulation of art from culture. The aesthetic critic recognizes that the excellence of modern art has been achieved at the expense of an unprecedented burden upon the artist—his isolation from public life. Hence modern art lacks the authority that art attained in stable and integrated cultures. The best art of our time is not representative; it embodies the triumph of the dedicated artist over the shortcomings of a culture. The aesthetic critic's chief social and cultural anxieties are not induced by the possible effects of social conditions upon literary works. Rather, they rise from his apprehension concerning the growing indifference of the culture to aesthetic value itself and the atrophy of the conditions that promote the survival of the arts.

The social pessimism of the contemporary critics may be attributed partly to their awareness of the present condition of letters. Though the absence of universally accepted standards precludes a single verdict on the quality of modern literature, critics are generally agreed on its status or—more precisely—the predicament of the writer. There is little doubt that the serious writer feels the disharmony between his own aims and those of his society as well as the inhibiting effect of this disharmony on his capability. Deprived of the spiritual support of his society, he must become an aberrant from its norms if he is to fulfill his potentialities. Social pessimism is not peculiar, however, to men of letters; nor can it be wholly ascribed to the malaise of the literary sensibility in our time, to its frustrations and discontents, its sense of alienation. The critic, inspecting fields other than literature, perceives that the literary situation is not only a symptom of social disintegration but part of a much larger process involving most human institutions. The student of society concentrates upon the centrifugal effect of disintegration upon institutions, the loss of coherence in the principal intellectual and practical activities of men; the literary man is more immediately struck by the effect upon sensibility. The diagnosis of the human condition is by now familiar: the disappearance of a central moral authority has deprived men of a common belief. Standards of value are merely arbitrary. Since symbols no longer have common reference, communication between the members of society is impaired. The individual is cast adrift, uncertain of his relation to a sodality and ignorant of his function.

It is generally believed that this process, whose full effect we are now experiencing, began with the Renaissance and has been accelerated by all the principal movements—religious, intellectual, and economic—that have since occurred in the Western world. The matrix of all elements that contributed to disintegration is the notion of the polarity of the individual and society.

The emergence of individualism and the correlative decline in prestige of communal institutions make up a topic too vast and complex to discuss here except as a general hypothesis. To represent schematically the proportion of individualistic and collective ingredients in the temper and thought of any period involves great risks. Though it is dangerous to postulate the homogeneity of a phenomenon so large and diverse as the romantic movement, there seems to be little doubt that the ideology of romanticism and of related nineteenth-century philosophies is the high-water mark in the development of individualism. The new ethos is most clearly manifest in the literary theory of the movement—its central concept of literature as a vehicle for expressing personal insight or emotion. Actually, in both practice and theory, the English romantic poets never discarded the traditional view concerning the reciprocal functions of literature and society. Despite his recoil from society, the romantic rebel was still fully implicated in it. Taken as a whole, nineteenth-century literature exhibits great social awareness; yet its central doctrine germinated a new alignment of writer and society, a radically new kind of literature that severed the traditional relationship.

The aftermath of romanticism was a series of movements (symbolism, art for art's sake, post-symbolism) that legitimatized the writer's alienation, assimilating it in aesthetic doctrine and practice. Edmund Wilson pronounced a valediction on the latest phase of the post-romantic movement in *Axel's Castle*. Wilson celebrates the stylistic and technical achievements of the post-symbolist writers, who explore new areas of experience

47

made available by the intensification of consciousness; yet he voices grave reservations about the defection of the highest literary talent from social responsibility. This phase of literature, he concludes, has exhausted its potentialities: the revival of literature depends upon the writer's voluntary abandonment of the "world of the private imagination" and return to the "life of society."

Axel's Castle possesses a documentary interest independent of its excellence as criticism. It signalized a turning point in the curve of literary sensibility. Though its subjects are writers who have been oppressed by the decadence of modern society, it is not in the least afflicted by social pessimism, a circumstance upon which its date—1931—has some bearing. This was the second year of a decade in which American criticism, indeed American intellectual life in general, exhibited an almost unbounded faith in the efficacy of social action to counteract disintegration and decay. The reaction against the romantic ideology was by now complete: man's collective function and nature had been reinstated—so fully, in fact, that in the same year Morris Cohen was prompted to say:

> A certain awe for the word *social* is one of the outstanding phenomena of current intellectual life. The triumphant elation and solace with which the social nature of man is announced and individualism denounced seems to presuppose the belief that previous generations were not aware of the fact that men live together.[2]

The prestige of the term "social" in literary criticism was at its height in the 'thirties, when Marxist criticism was in the ascendant. In retrospect, its successes seem less solid than they once did. The prominence of Marxist criticism, though short-lived, is remarkable for two phenomena: the enthusiasm with which a political doctrine was received in literary circles, and the emphasis placed upon literature and culture by what was mainly a political movement.

Society, or—more exactly—the idea of society, is the native element of Marxist thought. Although Marxist philosophy originally contained a humanistic strain that allowed for the ultimate importance of the individual, on the empirical level it treats society as the reality and the individual as an abstraction. It was the philosophic doctrine underlying the politics that made Marxism so attractive to middle-class intellectuals, particularly the literary critics. The doctrine dramatized history as a coherent, comprehensible social process. Its principal charm, however, was not interpretative but prophetic; according to the dialectic, contemporary disintegration was a necessary interlude in a larger and inevitable process of integration. This doctrine, embodied in a concrete political program, offered to the alienated intellectual a complete means of salvation. The conversion to Marxism, as has been often observed, has a far from superficial resemblance to religious conversion. Marxist faith was the antidote to pessimism and skepticism. Its cosmogony was the grand conception of historical movement. Its image of authority was the conception of social unity. Although the Marxist doctrine is deterministic, its politics provided the means of implementing faith by voluntary works.

For the twentieth-century literary sensibility, which had been repelled by the hypertrophy of individualism in modern literature, Marxism had a special attraction. Its historical theory, as applied to literature, reinforced an already widespread conviction of the indissoluble link between literature and society. Its literary program, founded upon this conviction, seemed to provide the alternative to anarchy and alienation by restoring to literature its proper social function. Marxist literary criticism, at least in its American phase, is an unstable fusion of these two elements—the one, a method of historical interpretation; the other, a didactic theory of literature.

49

This fusion reflects the ambiguity inherent in the whole Marxist position. Marxism is based on the hypothesis of historical determinism that accounts for all human activity in terms of a single motivation. The argument is that man is primarily a social being who derives his mental and moral constitution—his consciousness—from the social organization in which he participates. Social organization, in turn, is governed by economic organization—the control of the means of production. The most significant social fact about a man, therefore, is his economic class or stratum. Historical materialism, which postulates the determination of intellect, morals, and art by social forces, is augmented by dialectical materialism, which predicts the emergence of an integrated, classless society. The deterministic character of Marxist theory does not, however, preclude its fulfillment by a dynamic political program intent upon abetting the predetermined historical process. Since politics is inherently pragmatic and recalcitrant to theory, the Marxist intellectual adventure in America was soon subjected to the stresses of temporal politics.

Marxist criticism, considered as a technique of literary interpretation, is neither new nor revolutionary; it is an adaptation and expansion of nineteenth-century deterministic theories. Since its social coördinates are controlled by a rigorously logical philosophy of history, Marxist criticism seemed to have many advantages over Taine's environmental method. There is no fundamental disparity between the Marxist and any other sociological approach to literature. On the positive side, Marxist criticism in the United States both enlarged and refined the historical method. It threw light on the causative role of society in shaping American literature.

The vigor of Marxist criticism in the 'thirties resulted, not from an apparent superiority of objective and scientific techniques, but from the role assigned to literature in the regeneration of society. Marxist social philosophy implies a theory of culture, which forms the background of Marxist literary theory and its system of literary values. Culture, as understood in Marxist thought, is a narrower concept than that employed in current anthropological discourse. It signifies the nonmaterial superstructure—intellectual, moral, and aesthetic—that is generated by the material (economic) activities of a society. Whereas anthropology views the relations of society and culture as reciprocal, Marxist theory regards culture primarily as an effect of society. According to the latter view, the cultural products of a decadent society must be decadent; conversely, social regeneration will automatically bring in its wake a cultural renaissance. It does not follow that the individual is enjoined to a passive role, nor that the artist must resign himself to producing decadent art in the present. The artist may avert decadence by participating in the social process, identifying himself with its upward momentum. In short, he can counteract social and cultural determinism by voluntarily engaging in political action.

Marxist literary theory displays a similar dualism. The value of literature resides, on the one hand, in its accuracy as a sociological indicator, on the other, in its effectiveness as a political "weapon." In denying even a limited autonomy to culture and hence to literature, the more mechanistic Marxists renounce aesthetic criteria. Aesthetic matters, such as style, technique, and formal conventions, are reduced to their social origins. Literary judgment is based almost exclusively on ideological and moral criteria. In the latter, Marxist criticism represents no radical departure from the central tradition of criticism, which has been mainly nonaesthetic, moralistic, and utilitarian. Neither the method of Marxist criticism nor its literary theory, therefore, is a radical innovation. The only revolutionary element is its emphasis on the specifically political nature of ideas and morals; and this emphasis eventually destroyed the hegemony of Marxist criticism in the United States.

The foregoing account of Marxist critical principles is,

of course, vastly oversimplified. Despite great activity during a whole decade, this criticism achieved neither theoretical clarity nor a new approach. The fundamental disparity between its long-range and its short-range view of literature, for example, was never resolved. The exegetical and the hortatory functions of criticism were confused; the Marxist critics failed to align their view of contemporary literature and past literature in a unified perspective. Notwithstanding the doctrine of critical relativity, the "bourgeois" conception of aesthetic standards kept intruding itself.

Though all Marxist critics consented to the fundamental hypothesis of social determination, they differed about its application. The scattered literary pronouncements of Marx and Engels had furnished the precedent for a rather subtle, flexible interpretation of literature within the social frame of reference. In the 'thirties, however, the determinist doctrine often resulted in a rigidly mechanical account of literary origins. The more discerning exponents felt that an exclusively sociological approach could not cope with a phenomenon so multiform and complex as literature—that sociological techniques needed to be augmented by other insights. Efforts were made, for example, to assimilate the Freudian interpretation of literature into the Marxist system.

If Marxist criticism had been granted a period of political quiescence, it might have achieved a synthesis of its critical ideas, perhaps even consolidated its theory and method. The penalty it paid for political support was forfeiture of its independence and objectivity. Critics were subservient to the dictates of party politics; political orthodoxy replaced professional skill as a measure of critical achievement; political polemic eventually absorbed more attention than literature itself. Long before the general disillusion with Marxist social philosophy occurred, the most distinguished men associated with the movement, perceiving the threat to their integrity as critics, had broken with the Communist Party. The general disaffection with Marxism, of course, did not proceed from reservations about its literary aims, but from recognition of the meaning of its social philosophy as translated into political action.

Most of the American Marxist critics had not grown up in the tradition of revolutionary politics. They were converts from democratic liberalism who were already predisposed toward socialism—men discontented with the unbridled economic individualism of modern capitalism, its social inequities, its materialistic and standardized culture. In certain lights, the Marxist version of society seemed to be a logical extension of native political ideals within the context of industrial capitalism; further, the prospect of a collectivist society was exciting for those who deplored the atomization of contemporary civilization. The moment of apostasy occurred with the realization that Marxist social philosophy, emerging on the pragmatic plane, was terrifying in its absoluteness. It had become increasingly clear that socialization of the economy was to be achieved through complete subjugation of individual judgment to the collective whole, which turned out to be a political party, or—more accurately—an elite within the party, intent on preserving and propagating its own power. Individual judgment was an amenity to be held in abeyance until after the socialist society had been created. In short, the history of Marxist criticism in the United States is inextricably linked with the internal and international politics of the Soviet Union, particularly in the crucial years after 1936.

The honorific use of the term "social" declined along with the prestige of left-wing politics in American intellectual life. Interest in society, however, did not abate; nor was the hope of conferring order upon contemporary chaos abandoned. But the reaction from Marxist teachings increased the doubt about social means as the sole means of salvation. Judging from the example of the totalitarian state, rational unification was not equivalent to

53

genuine integration; the political regeneration of society might mean abrogating all other standards and values in favor of a single pragmatic standard. The situation of the artist in such a state was instructive; most of the former Marxist critics had not bargained for political control of culture.

Though society remains a principal extraliterary concern of criticism, the idea of society as it relates to literature has undergone subtle changes in the past two decades. Criticism is less positivistic than formerly and therefore less conducive to optimism. It is also less inclined to describe social phenomena in exclusively economic and political terms. Perhaps these modifications are best explained by the new importance of the concept "culture" in criticism; culture rather than society has come to be regarded as the proper medium in which to view the operations of literature. In the critical vocabulary, "culture" does not supplant "society"; only the notion of their relationship has been amended.

Marxist sociology, it will be recalled, defines culture as a secondary product of society; intellect and morals, religion and art, are determined by economic causes. Society, since all other values are derived from it, becomes the primary seat of value. To the anthropologist, culture is a much broader and much more elusive idea. It signifies the totality of social activities, whereas "society" becomes a neutral term denoting an organization of persons. Like Marxism, the latter point of view is deterministic: a society produces its culture. But that culture, having been produced, exists independently. It is viewed as a complex rather than as an aggregate of the activities of the individuals who compose a society. Culture is not wholly amenable to analysis, since the individual who is part of it cannot wholly apprehend it. In a sense, it is ultimately unknowable, being present as an unconscious element in the individual's means of apprehension. Though produced by society, it in turn shapes

54

that social organization and may be regarded as anterior to political and economic activities.

Cultural anthropology, from which these conceptions are derived, mistrusts reductive theories. Instead it provides the hypothesis of integration, according to which all elements of culture are functionally related. For one school of anthropologists the most important fact about a culture is the total configuration; according to this hypothesis, any single cultural element cannot be comprehended apart from the whole; nor can intellectual, moral, religious elements be abstracted from each other or from economic and political elements. The shift in emphasis from society to culture involves the recognition that literature, being infinitely complex, cannot be reduced to a scheme of extrinsic causes. Particularly the configurational hypothesis corroborates the critical position that suspects all unitary theories of literary causation.

It would be absurd to divide all contemporary criticism into two opposed camps—the aesthetic and the historical—and furthermore to identify the anthropological concept of culture with one and a positivistic concept of society with the other. Anthropological ideas have impressed many different kinds of critics, sociological critics included. Nevertheless, the shifting connotation of society is clarified if it is examined in relation to the polar extremes of contemporary criticism—the historical as represented by the Marxists, the aesthetic as represented by the new critics. The thesis of aesthetic criticism asserts that social information is irrelevant to the critical act; the aesthetic critic does not, however, deny the relevance of society to culture.

The branch of the new criticism most articulate on social and political subjects is the group associated with Southern agrarianism. Agrarianism comprises both a sociology and a politics. The politics, however, is curiously apolitical in that it is antipragmatic. The focus of political interest is culture—the life of society—rather than government—the formal mechanism of society. Culture in this context cannot be brought into being by an act of will, nor can it be reconstituted by voluntary planning. Hence the agrarian doubts that social change produces corresponding cultural changes. Whereas socialism envisages an overhauling of the social structure, drastic or gradual according to the politics of its adherents, the agrarian is conservative. Perceiving continuity to be the condition of culture, he is more devoted to permanence than to change. Yet his conservativism is not to be confused with defense of the *status quo*. He abhors both modern society and its culture; in their stead he predicates the traditional society, whose distinguishing virtue is the character of its culture. The traditional society is one that has produced a genuine culture.

The distinction between the positivist and the agrarian conception of society is further indicated by the contrast between state and community: for the agrarian the state is a political *organization*, created by fiat and sustained by conscious direction; the community is an *organism* that has evolved naturally, almost unconsciously, from the activities of a group sharing a common culture.

> Given plenty of time, and a space not too large for direct human intercourse, a real community develops from within outwards; it becomes a genuine expression of personal life. Its history and its physical form, down to the smallest detail, have idiosyncrasy and style. It holds a collective memory, a collective experience, which gradually become explicit as tradition or custom—all of it rooted, now as formerly, in the lives of persons associated with an actual earth.[3]

The organicist perspective confers upon community a unique order of reality; the life of the individual acquires meaning only as he participates in the collective reality. Thus the theory of the organic society has a certain affinity with Marxist collectivism in that both illustrate the widespread contemporary recoil from nineteenth-

56

century liberal individualism. But here the resemblance ends. For the Marxist, the supraindividual authority is vested in the collective will, that is, in society as pragmatically constituted. For the traditionalist, it resides in the body of custom handed down from generation to generation in a functioning community. In the latter's social philosophy the past is therefore an important dimension. Here the analogy of language is illuminating. Although language is a social construct, it is independent of society at any given moment. Language is in flux—it is constantly modified by society; yet its basic structure and identity are not appreciably modified by temporal events. The relation between language and culture, however, is more than analogical; language is the primary medium by which culture is transmitted. Social planning resembles the semantic approach that would reconstruct language by rational means. Traditionalist sociology might be compared, on the other hand, to the poetic use of language. T. S. Eliot, for example, defines the social role of poetry as identical with the poet's responsibility to his native language, both in advancing its capabilities and in preserving its purity (its integrity).

Marxist thought is oriented toward the future. It is confident that the issue of social reform is a better life—that a robust culture will be one result of a healthy society. This is the end that justifies the political means. The traditionalist critic, in his role as sociologist, rejects Marxist meliorism along with the liberal doctrine of progress. Confronted with the breakdown of culture in the modern world, he makes no political prescription for its restoration. The idea of the traditional society is founded upon the evidence of the past or—more precisely—upon an interpretation of history that is sometimes traced to Henry Adams's account of medieval culture. The social doctrine of the agrarians offers cold comfort in a time of distress. But even if their version of the past is doubted, their cogent analysis of present culture and the probity of their judgment are striking.

I have been discussing the opposition of Marxism and traditionalism; actually, they compete only on the level of doctrine. Whereas Marxist doctrine generated a great modern mass movement, the traditionalist social theory enlists only a handful of writers—men deeply concerned with the spiritual and intellectual conditions of modern life. Nor is it likely to win adherents, since it goes against the grain of our most cherished beliefs. Concerning the future of civilization, it is pessimistic or else resigned to decay. In the main it is antiequalitarian, preferring a graded or stratified society in which rank and function are hereditary. It favors decentralization in both government and culture, opposing to nationalism the doctrine of regionalism, to standardization the notion of diversity. Not impressed by technological progress, it advocates an agrarian society. Most important of all, it resists the whole momentum of modern thought toward scientific monism and affirms the indispensability of religious dogma embodied in a church as an element in culture.

Perhaps the most interesting fact about this social doctrine is that its most vigorous exponents are poets and critics, whose awareness of society was probably instigated by their experience as poets and critics. This information would serve to discredit their views with the layman, who prefers expert opinion. Ironically, in times of social and cultural disintegration, the poet or critic is likely to be the expert: he is compelled (unlike the writer in a stable society) to scrutinize and to question the assumptions of his age. It is axiomatic that a culture becomes conscious of itself only after it begins to decline. Another proposition might be appended: the artist becomes aware of his culture when he begins to probe the nature and status of his art—that is, when art itself becomes introspective.

The traditionalist sociology differs from other contemporary social theories in deriving its social structure from the requirements of an integrated culture. In such a culture each activity is informed by a single configuration that makes possible a fluent relation between all its various elements. An integrated culture releases the full creative potentialities of its members. But the condition of integration is stability, which in turn depends upon the transmission of culture from one generation to the next. The social organization held to be most favorable, if not indispensable, to propagating a tradition is both hierarchical and hereditary; but the emphasis is always on the tradition itself.

Tradition is the element that unites the poetic and social theory of this movement. Traditionalism is much more respectable now than it was a generation ago. Thanks to the dissemination of anthropological ideas, it is now generally recognized that the proportion of innovation to tradition in culture, language, and art is always slight no matter how great it may appear at the moment. This truth was not always evident; writers of the late nineteenth and early twentieth centuries liked to imagine that literature could be produced without antecedents. Their era was marked by wide experiment, exploitation of personal eccentricity, dissolution of traditional forms and traditional modes of feeling and judgment. For the poet nurtured in this era, the difficulties of achieving form and order were enormous; he could surmount them only by reconstituting the poetic tradition for himself. The resources of personal culture, though considerable, are limited. The poet perceived that beyond a certain point his problem could not be solved by personal effort—that it originated in the culture of his society.

The passage from the idea of tradition in poetry to the idea of the traditional society is not obscure. The relation of "traditionalist" criticism to a social hypothesis, however, cannot be so easily demonstrated, since the critical theory is based on a metaphysical assumption. This criticism has an aesthetic bias—the postulate that art, though not the artist, is autonomous. It therefore rejects the admissability of data concerning social or cultural origins, and affirms that aesthetic judgment can pertain only to evidence afforded by the work itself. One of its intentions is to avoid impressionism and relativism (both of which are partly attributable to modern disorder) by imposing a system of objective standards. Standards, whether aesthetic or moral, presuppose agreement within a group; the authority of a standard is proportional to the homogeneity of a society. The traditionalist critic, desiring to construct an authoritative and objective system, concludes that standards are relative to neither society nor culture but are in fact absolute—a subject that can be discussed only on the level of aesthetics or metaphysics.

3

The National Center

NATIONALITY will preoccupy the critic as long as literary works continue to be classified by their national origin; and the validity of the classification will not be disputed as long as language, the medium of literature, is important in criticism. In admitting the linguistic element as intrinsic, even the strictest advocate of induction must observe that the poet's idiom is derived from local and national idiom. The national category figures less prominently in aesthetic investigations of poems than in so-called historical criticism, which elucidates literary works with reference to their origin in time and space. Nationality, by far the commonest category in histories of literature, occupies one important tract in the total setting of works. Segregation according to nationalities does not of itself imply a plain brief for national literature; it may be merely a conventional solution of a problem in procedure. Literary nationalism, on the other hand, converts the national category into an active principle of composition, a criterion of value. In this perspective the preliminary condition of literary activity is a distinctive national culture; the value of a work is not only derived from nationality but also gauged by fidelity to the national culture.

Historically considered, literary nationalism has certain affinities with political nationalism. Its most vehement expressions have coincided with struggles for political independence, the argument for cultural autonomy enhancing the political argument. But beyond this parallel, generalizations are difficult in view of the radical singularity of the cultural and political situation in any one country. The idea of literary nationalism in

61

the United States, for example, originated in the Revolution, from which its momentum was received during much of the nineteenth century. American writers wished the nation to achieve a culture proportionate to its new political dignity. The idea of a distinctive American literature meant an explicit break with English literary tradition and usually embodied at least a remnant of revolutionary political sentiment; opponents of literary nationalism, like James Russell Lowell, were accused of being pro-British.

The political coördinates of literary nationalism in the United States today are far more obscure. For one thing, America's orientation with respect to British culture has shifted. Cultural autonomy now has reference to Europe as a whole. Hostility toward recent European art and ideas, which exists just beneath the surface of contemporary literary nationalism, can be correlated with a permanent isolationist strain in our politics. Further, the appearance of a fresh and powerful national movement in American letters, beginning after the First World War and culminating in the 'thirties, was connected with increasing political tension in Europe and with the growing imminence of another war.

After the First World War the sense of alienation from the home culture felt by American writers, many of whom had emigrated, was an isolated phenomenon. It had no counterpart in national life, but was limited to a group who resisted popular beliefs, tastes, and ideas. The contemporary nationalist movement in letters included writers who had previously participated in the international adventure. Now penitent and expiatory, they recoiled from a whole literary era and its attitudes. Vindication of the native involved reconciliation with the popular. Malcolm Cowley describes the shift in temper experienced by the returning expatriates.

> The exiles were ready to find that their own nation had every attribute they had been taught to admire in those of Europe. It had developed a national

type. . . . It possessed a folklore, and traditions, and the songs that embodied them; it had even produced new forms of art which the Europeans were glad to borrow. The exiles were preparing to embark on a voyage of discovery. . . . They saw the country of their childhood, which should henceforth be the country of their art. American themes, like other themes, had exactly the dignity that talent could lend them.[1]

Disillusionment with Europe, rediscovery of the native values, did not at first entail a conversion to political nationalism, for the new nationalist sentiment might be reconciled even with internationalist politics. Today, in its literary phase, American nationalism dissociates itself from political nationalism, which has been discredited intellectually, though it has lost none of its moral, emotional, or practical force. Literary nationalism concentrates on the benign effects of nationality—its creative role in culture.

Both as a critical doctrine and as a conscious or unconscious procedure in writing, literary nationalism is part of a broad philosophical, cultural, and religious effort to counteract the dislocations of modern intellect and sensibility. It participates in a general reaction against the body of ideas stemming from the eighteenth-century Enlightenment. It is allied with the agrarian, regionalist, folklorist, and primitivist movements that are also anti-uniformitarian, anticosmopolitan, antirationalist. In its specific field the nationalist doctrine of the 'thirties and 'forties attempted to reform, not so much the ideas as the leading temper of American letters, which in the preceding era had been distinguished by rootlessness, social irresponsibility, moral and intellectual anarchy.

The nationalist theory is basically "sociological"; for it, literary value and significance lie neither in aesthetic properties nor in "expressiveness," but in the utility of literature as a representation of society and as a medium for attaining social coherence. These assumptions are not

63

peculiar, of course, to the nationalist theory; they are shared by most practitioners of the historical method in criticism. The Marxist critics, notably, have employed some of the principal themes and arguments of literary nationalism, converting the widespread nationalist impulses of the era to their own ends. Originally founded upon an international outlook, both political and cultural, the Marxist movement as it gained momentum paid increasing attention to the national literature; for a time the Marxists seemed to monopolize the field of American literary history. In nominating realism as the approved mode or method, they drew close to a central tenet of literary nationalism: that an authentic literature adheres to the typical and the representative in national experience. Granville Hicks constantly applies this criterion in *The Great Tradition:* complete approval is withheld from the writer who falls short of being representative. Both Marxist and nationalist critics share the view that popular art alone embodies the authentic native elements in culture and thus constitutes the matrix of all art.

Apart from these concurrences, neither the tone nor the aims of the Marxists and nationalists were alike. Official Marxist criticism conformed both to a preconceived theory of literary causation and to current political necessity; in its version the authentic elements in the national culture were the ones that corroborated the political and artistic aims of the Communist Party. On the other hand, the literary nationalists, though by no means apolitical, were primarily moved by other than political ends. Their program was a much more modest one than the total reformation of society: they sought to rescue American writing from dependence upon the writer's personal vision or upon a narrow literary culture, accessible only to a self-ordained elite, by restoring literature to the national culture, hence to society as a whole. Their main effort, which should not be underestimated, has been to reclaim the materials required for the definition or redefinition of national culture. What concerns us here, however, is not the practical achievements of literary nationalism, but the underlying theoretical assumptions.

The theory itself lies partly within the scope of critical discourse proper, partly in the fields of history, anthropology, and sociology. It appropriates the main insight of historical method: that the literary work is a product of a specific cultural situation and can be best explained and evaluated as such. For the nationalist critic, culture is, of course, synonymous with national culture. He also presupposes that national culture—specifically, that of America—can be apprehended in a form available to the writer. His immediate problem—delimitation of the national culture—is complicated by the historic and geographic circumstances in which American culture evolved. A national culture has two dimensions: space and time. In the United States, culture developed within a relatively short period, yet extends over a vast territory. The disparity between these dimensions hampers a clear definition of American culture. In distinguishing between what is merely local and what is national, one criterion must be inclusiveness. The distinction must be made also between what is authentic or native and what is transitory and spurious. The test of authenticity, it might be supposed, is permanence: a culture must have roots (to use a cliché of contemporary criticism). It might be concluded, then, that the authentic elements in national culture are those created by the earliest settlers. This, the conventional view, is sometimes disputed on the ground that the earliest culture was colonial, not national, and that the only authentic culture was created in the frontier West. Regional tension is particularly evident in attempts to translate national culture into terms of a usable literary tradition.

Current literary nationalism is a product of liberal criticism, which in the 'twenties began to restore the submerged tradition of Concord and New York and to establish it as the core of a national literary culture. The liberal critics sought to remove the obscuring film deposited by the genteel tradition in American letters and to reveal the vigorous nationality of the original. In their canon, Emerson, Whitman, and Thoreau occupied the highest place; Melville and Hawthorne were accommodated with greater difficulty; Longfellow, Lowell, Holmes, Poe, and James were excluded, the last two for special reasons. The hierarchy remains fixed and is accepted by most nationalists. For a few of them, however, the first completely American writer is Mark Twain, and the origins of national culture lie where he found them—in the tradition and folkways of the frontier.

The doctrine of literary nationalism is derived, as already noted, from the customary use of the national category by the literary historian. He arrives at the category by two logical procedures: differentiation and identification. He establishes the validity of the national category, first by differentiating the literature of one nation from that of other nations; second by determining what attributes, common to the members of the class, confirm the identity of the class. The idea of literary nationalism occurred simultaneously with the beginnings of systematic literary history in the latter part of the eighteenth century. Both sprang from the romantic rebellion against cosmopolitanism in European letters—the cosmopolitanism that had been inaugurated by the Renaissance and brought to its peak by eighteenth-century neoclassicism. Romantic historicism denied the uniformity of human nature, the universality of culture; it is intimately connected with both romantic psychology and aesthetics. According to Irving Babbitt, these are facets of a single primitivist motive.

> Cultivate your genius, Rousseau said in substance, your ineffable difference from other men, and look back with longing to the ideal moment of this genius, the age of childhood, when your spontaneous self was not yet cramped by conventions or "sicklied

o'er with the pale cast of thought." Cultivate your national genius, Herder said in substance, and look back wistfully at the golden beginnings of your nationality when it was still naïve and "natural," when poetry instead of being concocted painfully by individuals was still the unconscious emanation of the folk. Herder indeed expounds primitivism along these lines into a whole philosophy of history.[2]

The contemporary case for cultural nationalism is argued on similar lines. In Rebecca West's *Black Lamb and Grey Falcon* there is the same emphasis upon cultural autonomy and upon the unique value of national essences:

> Here was the nationalism which the intellectuals of my age agreed to consider a vice and the origin of the world's misfortunes. I cannot imagine why. Every human being is of sublime value, because his experience, which must be in some measure unique, gives him a unique view of reality, and the sum of such views should go far to giving us the complete picture of reality, which the human race must attain if it is ever to comprehend its destiny. Therefore every human being must be encouraged to cultivate his consciousness to the fullest degree. It follows that every nation, being an association of human beings who have been drawn together by common experience, has also its unique view of reality, which must contribute to our deliverance, and should, therefore, be allowed a like encouragement of its consciousness. Let people then hold to their own customs, their own beliefs.[3]

The psychological phase of contemporary cultural nationalism does not abandon the original doctrine, but rather reinforces it with evidence drawn from the social sciences. The literary phase of contemporary nationalism is also indebted to its precursor. Its aesthetics follows the romantic bias, deprecating the conception of art as a controlled, disciplined craft and preferring spontaneity and the "natural" above all other qualities—hence its absorption with folklore and popular literature.

The appearance of a nationalist conception of cultural causation in Germany late in the eighteenth century was abetted by both literary and political circumstances. Earlier in the eighteenth century the native literary tradition had been eclipsed by a superficial cult of Gallic neo-classicism; its revival was stimulated, not only by the new idea of national culture, but also by awareness of the drive toward political unification. The ideas of Herder, Lessing, and the brothers Schlegel, transported to France by Mme de Staël, took firm root in that stronghold of classicism. Taine's *Art of the Netherlands* and *History of English Literature* established the direction that literary history and historical criticism were to follow for nearly a century. As Mary Colum demonstrates in *From These Roots*, the genealogy of the leading ideas in contemporary historical criticism can be traced directly to Herder and Lessing on the one hand, to Taine and Sainte-Beuve on the other.

American criticism, except for the dissenting aesthetic school, has been governed mainly by one or more of the modes of historical criticism: the psychological, the sociological, the national. Until rather recently our critics have treated as axiomatic the notion that the spiritual and psychological history of a people may be constructed from their literary and artistic products and, conversely, that literary and artistic production are determined by national characteristics. Aesthetic criticism does not actually try to supplant one theory of literary causation by another; it subverts the historical approach by ruling out of criticism the whole topic of causation. The antecedents of a literary work admissible in criticism are considered to lie strictly within the literary realm, that is, in precedent works. The nationalist critics sought to establish a national tradition; the liberals and Marxists, a political one. The new critics have constructed, according to their own criteria of authenticity or orthodoxy, a literary tradition with theological overtones. This tradition embraces Dante, the Jacobean dramatists, the metaphysical poets, the French symbolists and others. It has a certain resemblance to the self-conscious "Classical Tradition" that has operated continuously in European letters since the Renaissance; in fact, it is deliberately conceived as the foundation of a new classical movement.

The "Classical Tradition" itself received its severest blow from romantic literary and cultural theory, which emphasized the relation between national literature and language. Modern linguistic investigation apparently strengthens the nationalist thesis; it discloses that the language of a social group transcends the communicative function by serving as the repository and vehicle for common modes of thought, feeling, and behavior, in fact, for what we now regard as culture. Inasmuch as the writer employs the medium of language, he is involved in a tradition that extends far beyond linguistic technique into the living experience of the group. To restore the native tongue was a powerful motive, both political and cultural, of nationalist movements in countries where the language of a conqueror had been imposed. Aside from a few extremists who urged the establishment of a new language, the first cultural nationalists in the United States were compelled to abandon language as one of the differentia of American literature. Uncertainty about the cultural role of language explains the ambivalent attitudes toward the national literature in the nineteenth century. On the one hand, it seemed both wise and expedient to assign American letters an honorable though subsidiary place in the great tradition of English letters. This point of view was voiced as late as 1913 in John Macy's *The Spirit of American Literature*, which specified a category of Anglo-Saxon literature. That solution, on the other hand, was anathema to the militant nationalist: he saw in it an abject colonial timidity, which underrated the potentialities of a young and vigorous nation. Literary nationalism in the nineteenth century had to be satisfied with potentiality rather than achievement. When Whitman, the first writer to meet the nationalist specifications, finally appeared, his eccentricities were more evident than his representative qualities. His national stature was not recognized until the twentieth century; by that time literary nationalists did not have to deal solely with expectations.

Few critics today doubt that the existing corpus of American writing is differentiated enough to stand as a national literature. Ironically, considering the embarrassment of earlier critics on this score, its distinctiveness is mainly linguistic. Also ironic is the fact that much contemporary writing celebrated in Europe for its American qualities (especially style) is deplored by the nationalist critics as false to the native tradition. There is no doubt about either the existence of an American language or its use in literature. Though the main British attitude toward "American" is still defensive, perceptive English critics have attributed the distinction of recent American writing to the freshness and strength of the idiom. It is completely credible also that American writing has evolved a native style apart from idiom.

> That we have a national prose is patent. It is characteristically marked by a sinewy and simple syntax, swift rhythmic periods, brilliant informality of manner, and freshness (often degenerating into the grotesque) of figure and diction. These qualities tend to differentiate prose here from prose in Great Britain.[4]

The entire linguistic question, as it relates on the one hand to national culture, on the other to style and diction, is important in criticism, particularly as it bears upon the intricate and subtle dependence of poetic diction on the idiom and rhythm of speech. But preoccupation with dialect, folk speech, and the vernacular by no means exhausts the linguistic properties of poetry or prose. In his recent essay on Milton, T. S. Eliot points out that the need to revivify poetic diction by means of the resources of current speech is perennial but not absolute. The poet sometimes needs to immerse himself in "poetic" diction, in the language of artifice wrought by poetry. Obviously the cultivation of the vernacular is essential to an emergent national literature. Yet does the brilliance of Mark Twain's prose warrant the proscription of Henry James's mandarin style from our tradition?

The discovery and elucidation of certain differentiae have helped clarify the relation of American works to culture. Clearly the identity of American letters is not only a matter of intuitive perception; it can be demonstrated objectively with respect to both "extrinsic" and "intrinsic" attributes. In labeling a critic "nationalist," however, we impute to him a point of view more positive than the recognition of national idiosyncrasies in literature. Such a critic is convinced, first, that national idiosyncrasy is a warrant of the creative force in national culture; second, that nationality is a prime criterion of literary value. The creativeness of national cultures can be deduced, not from national differentiae, but from the identity of national traits. Since a culture comprises a nearly infinite number of seemingly discrete elements, the critic must demonstrate the principle according to which they are integrated; in other words, he must prove the homogeneity of the culture.

The most familiar means of indicating homogeneity is the concept of national character. It is the *donnée,* for example, of Van Wyck Brooks's literary theory. In his early work Brooks attributed the past defects of American writing to the writers' acquiescence in inferior culture; he also maintained that a great literature could become great only by expressing the genuine national quality—the essence that had somehow been betrayed by a materialistic civilization.

A *focal centre*—that is the first requisite of a great people. And by this I do not mean the sense of a national or imperial destiny which has consolidated the great temporal powers of history. I mean that national "point of rest" ... that secure and unobtrusive element of national character, taken for granted, and providing a certain underlying coherence and background of mutual understanding which Rome, for example, had in everything the name of Cato called up. ... "National character" is only the perhaps too conscious equivalent of this element in which everything admirably characteristic of a people sums itself up, which creates everywhere a kind of spiritual teamwork, which radiates outward and articulates the entire living fabric of a race.[5]

The notion of cultural homogeneity, whether it be conveyed by the metaphor of national character, national mind, or national genius, implies the corollary view that nationality, being unitary, is corrupted by exotic elements.

Is it not the glory of Lessing that he established a sort of norm of the German character ... ? Was it not, in fact, the great work of Lessing ... that he purged the German mind of all its exotic elements and grounded its literature in the firm subsoil of its own nature?[6]

Brooks's preoccupation is neither singular nor willful; the idea of national character has been present in historical thinking at least since the time of Herodotus, and its relevance to literary history has been thoroughly ratified in the method of Taine. Employed by Taine and his successors as an objective instrument, it bears no taint of chauvinism, as the following passage illustrates.

The day has come, it seems, when the broad facts of literary history can be more closely connected not only with physical and social agents, but with a moral one—namely, the development of the national mind itself. ... From this point of view it is possible to regard two centuries and a half of

English literature as a succession of moments in the history of the English mind, each stage of which obeyed a craving for novelty and contrast, while consciously or unconsciously preserving the accumulated capital of all previous experiences. Such, in fact, is the normal development of that collective personality, a nation.[7]

The idea of a collective psyche, a version of the *Volksgeist* of romantic cultural theory, is intimately bound up with the organicist perspective in nineteenth-century thought, which informed, among other things, Coleridge's conception of the structure of poetry. In the aesthetics of later romantic writers like Emerson and Whitman, the organic structure of poems was regarded as evidence that poetic composition is essentially spontaneous and even automatic. This theory was, of course, apposite to the nationalist view of literary causation: according to it, literature can be interpreted as a direct product and representation of national life and national character.

It is now fashionable to dismiss collective personality or corporate consciousness as a fiction, untenable on either logical or biological grounds. The idea, however, still retains potency; far from being readily disposed of, it is being restated in empirical terms. The ancient, uncritical notion of the identity of groups is borne out by the anthropological approach to culture and to social psychology. Kardiner and Linton's hypothesis of "basic personality structure" avoids the fallacy inherent in the idea of group consciousness; it obviates the need of accepting the doctrine of race memory or the collective unconscious.

The basic personality type for any society is that personality configuration which is shared by the bulk of the society's members as a result of the early experiences they have in common. It does not correspond to the total personality of the individual but rather to the projective systems, or ... the value-

73

attitude systems which are basic to the individual's personality configuration. . . . The term *basic personality structure* was chosen to obviate the lack of clarity in the terms group, national, or social character, because a group can no more have a common character than it can have a common soul or pair of lungs.[8]

Cultural nationalism need no longer, then, be associated with belief in a national mystique or the reality of a supraindividual mentality. According to the anthropological view, the unity of a culture inheres in its basic pattern, its configuration. The cultural anthropologist has discarded the idea of an original essence that determines the authenticity of cultural traits; he allows for the variety and independence of cultural activities. The identity and unity of a culture subsist in the manner in which the activities are related to each other and to the whole complex of such relationships—that is, to the configuration. The configurational hypothesis, moreover, explains how a culture can assimilate elements that are neither original nor indigenous.

Sometimes anthropological insights are directly appropriated to literary history.

"A genuine continuity, an intrinsic significance, can be arrived at only by avoiding any definition of the cultural form as the sum of cultural elements. There must be a uniform cultural gestalt from which the concrete objective expressions of the culture draw their meaning. The unity of such generic, all-embracing pattern is intelligible only as a psychological unity. . . . The mentality of an ethnic group becomes audible in its folk songs, one might say, just as it becomes visible in its arts and crafts." [Heinz Werner, *Comparative Psychology of Mental Development*] Substitute "literature" for "folk-songs" and "nation" for "ethnic group," and we have in this passage, in contrast to the theories of economic determinism, Freudian psychology or

Marxist literary history, the only concept of national culture which a literary historian can hope successfully to use.[9]

So far as criticism admits the relevance of extraliterary information and investigates the genesis of works, the relation between literature and culture is important. Its importance is further enhanced if the homogeneity of culture is demonstrated. Contemporary anthropological theory, however, does not recommend that the configurational hypothesis be applied indiscriminately to the culture of modern complex societies. It no longer takes for granted the alleged homogeneity of preliterate societies—a staple of earlier anthropology. Without minimizing the methodological value of the configurational approach for students of culture, I doubt whether the question of literary causation can be entirely solved by anthropological techniques, that is, by transposing "nation" and "ethnic group," "literature" and "folk songs."

Aware of the extraordinary difficulties involved in discovering a regulative principle in complex modern cultures, the professional anthropologist or sociologist is cautious on this score; he rarely treats more than a small segment of the whole. The ambitious formulations of the world historians are notoriously suspect. No wonder, then, that American culture proves intractable to both analysis and definition—more so perhaps than any other contemporary culture. To advert once more to its singularity: American culture is coterminous neither with the life of the republic (that is, with nationality) nor with the history of the New World. The original settlers brought with them the highly differentiated, sophisticated culture of post-Renaissance Europe. They lacked a monolithic and continuous native tradition reaching back into a remote past, when culture and society were both presumably homogeneous. A native configuration, if it actually exists, must have taken shape later on. For the cultural historian the crucial questions are: at what point

75

did American culture become national and cease to be something else?; what are the signs of the national configuration, and where are they primarily evident—in political organization, in religion, in economy, in the physical terrain, in art?

An objective study of American writing as a residual index of culture might provide the surest approach. Although several literary historians have announced this aim, they have not fully achieved it, having employed categories drawn from nonliterary (notably political) history. In other words, cultural history is subsumed in political or social history, as in the familiar division of American literature into three stages—colonial, provincial, national. Because the political phase of American culture has been more vocal and more dramatic than other phases, there is a general tendency to identify the national Gestalt with political experience—to designate our culture, in effect, as essentially democratic, equalitarian, pragmatic, and idealistic. This is by far the commonest formulation in the literary histories of the present century. Without underestimating the preponderant role of politics and social organization in modern culture, I suspect its inadequacy; for culture, as the anthropologists have taught us to view it, includes areas of thought, feeling, and behavior that cannot be reduced to political or even social motives. The literary nationalists who would construct a national tradition on a base of political awareness or social sentiment are likewise oversimplifying: they ignore whole regions of the literary imagination beyond the scope of politics and social philosophy. The reductive propensity of American criticism is exemplified in its treatment of the deeply rooted puritan strain in our culture and character. Translated into either political and economic or psychological terms, puritanism occupies an extremely uncertain status in the various designs for a national tradition. But it has seldom been reckoned with on the plane of religion or morals.

A paradox in contemporary speculation is the belief that the heterogeneous elements in American culture were not thoroughly fused and integrated until rather recently—that a genuinely national literature did not come into being until our own time.

> We stayed semi-colonial, still experimental, still largely local until the first World War brought to a nation, now a conglomeration of races, though still English in tradition and speech, a consciousness that literature, whatever its tradition, had a job to do in finding voices for a vast country. What had been a new world geographically speaking was now, for the first time, perhaps, realized as a new world of human experience. From 1920 on the vast majority of the best American books in creative literature could have been written only in America. . . . The background of our rich and varied history is the unifying factor. . . . I do not refer to . . . passionate nationalism . . . but to that deeper experience of a soil, a sky, and a sense of national or racial unity which one finds behind all great literature.[10]

The paradox here is that the diversity of American experience constitutes the unity of American culture; this point of view in effect denies the traditional basis of culture and abandons the criterion of homogeneity. The central problem of cultural analysis is, of course, the discernment of unity in diversity. The anthropologist would not accept the hypothesis that a unified culture can result from the accumulated diversified experience of a society. Instead, he maintains that the unifying principle should be sought in the unity of experience (custom).

The endeavor to perceive the lineaments of a national culture in its more sophisticated forms—its political and religious institutions, its formal intellectual and literary activities—is constantly frustrated, since no critic can unify such diversity, such inherent contradictions. The alternative method is to detect the shape of a culture in its simple, irreducible elements and only later to cor-

77

relate these with the more complex forms. The nearest literary equivalent to anthropology is the study of folklore. Disinterested folklore research is, of course, not committed to a nationalist point of view. Like scholarly literary history, it issues from the romantic revival in Germany, where the first systematic folklore studies were applied to liberate German letters from a slavish imitation of foreign models. This meant a return to indigenous materials created before the neoclassic ideal had cast its spell on European culture—on the one hand, a return to the native epics; on the other, to the ballads and folk tales that had been preserved, unsuspected, in the countryside while the formal literature had been evolving in town and at court. (The exploitation of folk material had political as well as cultural ramifications, since folk art, in contrast with formal aristocratic art, could be represented as the authentic product of the people.) In European letters, folklore and nationalism have been intimately associated as late as our own era. They were indissolubly linked, for example, in the Irish literary renaissance, which endeavored to reclaim the national tradition in a poetry and drama founded upon folk speech, folk belief, and a native mythology.

The literary theory of the Irish movement has profoundly influenced American literary nationalism—not always with positive results, since the conditions of our culture are nearly as enigmatic in folklore as in other aspects. Experts dispute whether we possess a body of native folklore large and significant enough to serve a native tradition. But even if we do, the nationalists' preempting of folklore is seriously contested by the regionalists. The latter argue the factitiousness of "native" and "culture" applied on a national scale. According to their argument, in the United States the region, rather than the nation as a whole, constitutes a unit corresponding to a national culture in Europe. Notwithstanding these and other reservations concerning American folklore, folk materials provide a sound basis for objective study of a culture and are perhaps the only medium for discovering its configuration. Folklore is more closely integrated with group experience, group emotions, and group attitudes than the self-conscious literature, art, and philosophy of sophisticated societies, which, as already observed, are refractory to anthropological investigation. It is precisely the unconscious element in folklore (the spontaneity so highly regarded by romantic critics) that makes it valuable to the student of culture.

The work of Constance Rourke is among the few systematic efforts to relate American art to its cultural context. Unfortunately, only a few fragments of her projected study of American culture were achieved; but they do reveal both its method and direction. "In the large, the problem for the American artist is a cultural problem, and it is only through a full appropriation of our cultural tendencies that the sound frame of native reference, which major painting requires, can be provided."[11] Though this looks like a nationalist program, it must not be inferred that her work belongs in the category of literary nationalism, since the statement refers specifically to painting. Miss Rourke deliberately eschews literary nationalism; according to her bold but tentative *aperçu,* the native aesthetic genius is probably not literary at all. She surmises that America, though capable of great individual works, cannot produce a body of literature that may be called national.

Miss Rourke's investigations were controlled by the idea of cultural configuration, which she derived from Ruth Benedict's *Patterns of Culture* and adapted to her own purposes.

> It is the whole configuration in the particular period which is important, with its special tenacities, currents of thought, contagions of feeling, its dominant arts whether they are polite or impolite, practical or impractical, whether they slip over surfaces in tran-

sitory popular forms or become rooted as patterns
of the folk-imagination or, more broadly, of social
imagination.[12]

In applying this concept, Miss Rourke recognizes that
the configuration does not usually appear on the surface
of cultural products. In penetrating to the cultural experience (the social life) beneath the level of economic
and political activity, she discovers sources largely ignored by critics whose outlook had been shaped by the
narrow prejudices of the "genteel" attitude. This attitude
associated art with the insignia of social rank; reserved
it for a limited, specialized class; surrounded it with an
aura of inaccessibility; admired only the foreign and
despised the homespun; recognized only what Miss
Rourke calls the "peaks" of cultural achievement; ignored the great mass of artistic production indispensable
to the appearance of masterpieces; indulged in the historical snobbery that terminates painting with the Ital-
ian Renaissance and regards everything subsequent as
decadent; and finally, relegated art to the museum and
the academy. Without missing the all-important distinction between fine art and folk art, Miss Rourke reveals
their essential continuity both with each other and with
the whole social and cultural pattern.

Her general thesis is nationalist or (to use a term less
weighted with political connotations) nativist. Her con-
tention that the core of culture is indigenous is squarely
situated in the historical method.

> With enough European schooling and a sufficiently
> large number of civilized contacts, it has been
> hoped that esthetically we might at last begin to
> develop. We had only to catch up with Europe . . .
> by diligent study. This is to disregard the ways in
> which cultures have grown and been sustained in
> the past. Most cultures have at some time been sub-
> ject to foreign influences, but surely the center of
> growth of any distinctive culture is to be found

within the social organism and is created by peculiar and irreducible social forces.[13]

There is nothing here that is not acceptable to most
literary nationalists. Her originality lies in perceiving
that the native quality resides, not in the subject matter
of art, but in the form. If the reverse assumption were
true, much American painting and almost all American
writing would be automatically national. Miss Rourke
does not believe that the artist has acquitted his cultural
function merely by using native materials.

> The painting of Grant Wood, with its American
> types and regional backgrounds and themes, has all
> the orthodox elements of a native art, but this
> painter many times used superficial and transient
> elements of the American subject without touching
> its core. . . . In our own time Marin has overpassed
> the demands of subject and has used that turn
> toward purity of color and abstraction, which have
> a secure place in our traditions, with a humorous
> assertion of personal idiosyncrasy which anyone
> familiar with forms of our character will immedi-
> ately recognize.[14]

Her work, being mainly exploratory, does not enunciate
in a formula the core of American culture; we learn only
that it exists in an element of the native character
formed by the environment. Thus the formal tradition
incorporated in the style and method of Charles Sheeler
derives from that fastidious sense of craftsmanship
exhibited in early colonial objects and architecture.
Whether the environmental hypothesis can illuminate
literature as well as it does painting is dubious. Aside
from her suggestive essays on the sources of an early
native dramatic tradition in the sermons of Jonathan
Edwards and the Indian treaties, it is not pressed hard
or developed.

Most writing, of course, bears the marks of a locality;
but real evidence of an inherent compulsion in the liter-

ary process, whereby the writer's *total* handling of his materials is determined by a particular environment, would be pertinent to nationalist criticism. The theory itself seems applicable only to a primitive stage of literature and, as might be expected, is seriously proposed only by the thoroughgoing primitivist. Mary Austin, for example, situates the centrality of experience (the basis for a national art) in the individual's rapport with his immediate physical environment. Her point is that the actual art forms employed by American artists were imports—that the best efforts of American art in the past resulted from forced, artificial graft of native modes of thought and feeling upon alien forms. The consequence was a stultifying gap between the genuine elements in native expression and the efforts of serious artists. To heal the breach, she pleads for a poetry that "shall go down within the nation till it reaches the basic rhythms, the stroke of the paddle or the curves of the landscape, the sequence of the weather and the crops."

No doubt this represents a sentimental version of even the most primitive kinds of poetry; but it does illustrate, in extreme form, a persistent motive in literary nationalism—namely, atavism. Here the nationalist doctrine is true to type, that is, to its romantic origins. The reasonable hypothesis that culture develops from a central core initiates the search for essential, irreducible elements. Interest in authenticity and homogeneity is thus stimulated and leads ultimately to the position that the "nonessential" elements actually disrupt the homogeneity of culture. Since homogeneous cultures exist only in the past or in contemporary survivals of "noncivilized" societies, nationalism in its romantic phase hopes to recapture the native, primitive purity there and restore it to present use. The underlying aim is neither critical nor historical, but evangelical; it seeks to regenerate literature by reviving the spirit and values of folk literature, or—more specifically—folklore. This movement is differentiated from both literary history and literary anthropology. In its more extreme manifestations it is actually unhistorical, since it ignores both the stratified structure of modern cultures and the development of literature in relation to that structure.

Contemporary interest in folklore and in the popular elements in art has been wholly salutary; it has counteracted the snobbish "genteel" evaluation of art. Yet it is one thing to perceive the absolute beauty and significance of folk art and to acknowledge also its contributions to formal or sophisticated art; it is quite another thing to set up a division wherein the conventional attitude toward the two modes of art is reversed. In their contempt for the products of high culture, in their anti-intellectualism, in their animus toward the foreign as foreign and the modern as modern, the adherents of folk art reveal their own form of snobbishness. They exclude from the native canon the elements making for technical finish—emphasis on formal values, subtlety and complexity of expression—all of which they attribute to the decadent culture of Europe. This exclusion is based partly upon a conception of native folk art as a direct, immediate expression of communal life unhampered by artifice—an art that remains simple, spontaneous, instinctive, and even crude. Here is a highly sentimental version of folk art, some of which does indeed display simplicity, spontaneity, and innocence. Like primitive art, however, folk art is sometimes extremely conventionalized, abstract, and complex, displaying a considerable degree of technical competence. Yet the belief persists that folk art embodies the elemental, essential properties of art, from which the sophisticated art of urban societies represents a falling away in power. If sophisticated art happens to display this primary power, it is often labeled "folk art," a procedure that adds to the difficulties of definition and obscures the values of genuine folk art.

Although self-conscious and deliberate primitivism is aberrant rather than normal in contemporary criticism, a strong primitivist bent has been present in American letters almost from the beginning. An examination of doctrinal primitivism can therefore illuminate some aspects of criticism that are not primarily or intentionally primitivist. The basis of all primitivist ideas is, of course, the antinomy of mind and nature, which produces an indefinite series of opposites: reason and emotion, ethos and pathos, convention and spontaneity, form and substance. Preoccupation with "nature" as physical landscape and as primordial culture, moreover, is bound to have regionalist affiliations in the United States. The strongest case for primitivism has been made by regionalists, particularly those of the West and Southwest, who advocate a "hard" primitivism as distinguished from the "soft" one of the Southern agrarians. The manifesto of this movement is B. A. Botkin's *The New Regionalism* (1929).

> Far different in character from the early local color school is the New Regionalism growing out of the new "renaissance of wonder," which is retrospective rather than prophetic, with an insatiable curiosity about the past of history and tradition. As in the English Romantic movement, America is now developing a true historical sense, realizing that only in the light of the past can one understand one's environment. . . . As a result, in its naturism, it is breaking away from facile impressionism and mechanical realism to the "subliminal influences" of terrain and atmosphere; away from the humanitarian ideal of the "common man" to the commonality of the folk and a "national background of ideas." In seeking the support of a "native cultural tradition," it is assisted by a new school of literary history and criticism that is likewise in search of native standards.[15]

Botkin's debt to Irish literary theory is evident in the series—folklore, ritual, and myth.

> In the common stack of speech, custom, and belief,

84

from which [regionalism] derives a native imagery and symbolism, it is finding the universality and simplicity without which art degenerates into mere journalism and technique. In the homely, actual "observer's art" and in the natural poetry of legend and superstition are the solid bases in fact and mythology that supplement and balance each other. Seeking to unite the streams of written and oral tradition it is creating a genuine American myth and fable; and by setting the myth-making instinct at work upon actual characters it is creating an American saga and epic. . . . This literature bases its appeal primarily on the ideal of a Golden Age, of which the folk and the frontier are the last repository . . . the Golden Age of primitive art and ritual, of pagan fantasy and mysticism, with taboos and symbols embedded in the folk consciousness."[16]

The ethnological style of this passage is becoming more and more familiar in contemporary criticism. The doctrine advanced, however, has very little in common either with the British school of literary archaeology that stems from Frazer and Murry or with the mythological techniques employed by such critics as Kenneth Burke and William Troy. The latter have no wish to minister to modern literature in its infirmities, but desire rather to convert scientific knowledge of myth into an analytical instrument for explaining all literature in terms of universal, primordial elements. The salient difference between the empirical use of myth as a critical method and self-conscious primitivist movements is the proposition that literature of the mythical order can be deliberately created or re-created in the present. The primitivists fail to recognize what W. B. Yeats eventually accepted as inevitable—that the problem is cultural, not literary.

The operation of primitivist ideas in literary criticism is clearly exhibited in T. K. Whipple's *Study Out the Land*. Whipple's initial proposition is the breach between the modern artist and his public and the resulting sterility of modern art: "Meanwhile, becalmed upon this windless sea of neglect, the artists and their hangers-on degenerate into connoisseurs and virtuosos and technicians, and quarrel over the functions and purposes of their several arts, and lament the crassness of the modern age." A solution is offered in the "potent image."

> Only potent images have value for art. The most valuable are those which are racial or national, or still better, universal. . . . Perhaps the nearest that America has come to such "potent images" is in Lincoln or Jesse James—the mythical, not the historical figures—or in the Indian.[17]

In Whipple's criticism may be traced a growing alienation from the major figures in twentieth-century American literature, whose failures he had recounted in *Spokesmen,* and a compensatory attraction toward the regional writers and popular writers like Zane Grey.

> Nor is it very difficult to see what the trouble is: by and large, the better American writers are too highbrow. They find Henry James more interesting than Jesse. Following in the train of European leaders, they have spent their time hunting the exact word. . . . They have abandoned themselves to trying to be subtle, minute, and accurate.[18]

As a refuge from the artistic legacy of Flaubert and Henry James, Whipple proposes the myth of a heroic age that will preserve for a complex culture the values of a simpler world.

> In all the talks about the West—or the frontier, for the terms are synonymous—and about how it has "formed our character as a nation" for better or worse, one aspect of the subject has been neglected: its value as a national myth or symbol.[19]

Whipple voices here an extreme and rather desperate version of an idea that has haunted American writers for nearly a century—the idea of a literature of affirmation, of heroic proportions, that would embody the entire

86

national experience rather than the experience of an individual sensibility. We see the idea at work in the ambition of Hart Crane and Thomas Wolfe to master the epic and heroic modes. Almost inevitably the idea terminates in nostalgia for the West that is a symbol of lost innocence.

The whole question of nationality in literature and its proper evaluation is subject to the perplexities attending all literary questions of a very general nature: the difficulty of adequate definition and the difficulty of standards. Literary or cultural nationalism is complicated by its existence on three separate though not always distinct levels: literary history, cultural history, and literary criticism. Its validity is not necessarily identical in all branches.

If the contribution of literary history to the understanding of literature is accepted pragmatically, irrespective of its instability as a genre, the value of the national concept must also be recognized. The segregation of literature according to national categories illuminates, quite apart from any theory of cultural integration, the coherence of literary activity within the national framework. But the literary historian is rarely content to remain a mere chronicler; the very use of the national context invites him to exhibit the relation between literature and other activities in the context and to construct hypotheses concerning that relation. The principal ones—both deterministic—are social determinism and the theory of cultural configuration, the one stressing the immediate social environment, the other stressing inherent psychological traits transmitted by a culture. In practice, the cultural approach is less given to reductive reasoning than the sociological; but, being mainly apposite to primitive cultures, it is inferior as a historical method.

Neither theory, obviously, need be confined within national boundaries; each may be applied on either a

wider or narrower scale. It is easier to justify the unity of
the United States on political or economic grounds, for
example, than on cultural grounds. The presumption of
an organic national culture is controverted, not only by
regionalist sociology, but by other contemporary sociologies that posit the unity of Euroamerican or Western
culture. Constance Rourke, following a clue provided by
Worringer's thesis of the absolute and radical distinction
between the Greek and Byzantine art styles—a distinction based on a difference of artistic forms, intentions,
and standards arising from two contrasting, integrated
cultures—infers the existence of a native configuration.

> Now whether or not so positive a contrast exists
> between our artistic intention and that of European
> groups, the fact remains that our "configuration,"
> either socially or geographically is not the Euro-
> pean "configuration." It would seem obvious that
> our art, if we are to have one, must spring from the
> center rather than the periphery of our culture. . . .
> Yet our criticism on the whole has considered Euro-
> pean art in the absolute terms to which Worringer
> refers, and has related American art to this as if no
> basic differences existed between the groups of
> civilizations.[20]

Although the idea of a configuration is important for
sociology and for the history of culture, its relevance to
literature is problematical. In our own culture at least,
the value of literary works is traditionally considered to
inhere in their uniqueness. It is not necessary to subscribe
to an aesthetic nominalism to perceive that both sociology and cultural history are intent upon discovering the
generic attributes of cultural products and are therefore
devoted to the typical and the representative. The sociologist can dispense with literary values as extraneous
to his purpose, which is just as well served by the inferior
work. As a matter of fact, the "sub-literature" and mass
art of modern industrial societies are probably more
accurate sociological indices than their belles-lettres.

88

The dilemma of the literary historian is that his criteria cannot be merely quantitative. The ambiguity involved in historical and cultural studies of literature, inasmuch as they lie somewhere between criticism and sociology, accounts for the common attribution of value to the representative aspects of literature on the one hand and to its popular appeal on the other.

The literary nationalist judges the value of a work by its conformity or fidelity to a national archetype—the American spirit or American experience. On the other hand, although the popular attributes of a work may be felt intuitively to inhere in the work itself, their objective existence can be demonstrated only in terms of public response to the work. Popular art is a very elusive category. It is a modern conception required by the increasing complexity of artistic activity in modern industrial and democratic societies, but it is not easily defined with respect to either art or society. Primitive folk art is often, though not quite accurately, regarded as the unitary art of primitive society, serving the needs of all its members. The next stage is that of the literate culture where the diversification of society brings about a division between urban art and folk art, the latter being a continuation of primitive art, the former familiar to us as the great classic art of integrated, organic cultures. The process of fission is accelerated after the Renaissance: folk art in the original sense is no longer created; art is deliberately produced for specialized publics; industrialism and universal literacy give rise to a new phenomenon—a mass-produced commercial art; the terms "high-brow," "low-brow," and finally "middle-brow" are superimposed on the previous categories.

From a strictly sociological point of view, commercialized mass art should be regarded as the popular art of our time; but to the nationalist critic the term "popular art" signifies something else. Defined negatively, it is that art whose characteristics are conspicuously antithetical to those of the advanced art prized by literary elites. Such

89

an art work usually displays great emotional power or profound sentiment. Its technical defects are obvious; the style and diction may be clumsy, or the theme or plot extremely conventional, almost a stereotype. Nevertheless the public, in defiance or ignorance of expert critical opinion, persists in cherishing the work, which thus acquires the status of a "popular classic." How can such a work be classified?

A concrete example is *Uncle Tom's Cabin,* a social tract of almost unprecedented power that has never lost its hold on the popular imagination. By any sociological standard it is a "great" work; but this valuation is contradicted by most critical estimates, thus posing a nice problem for the literary historian as critic and cultural historian.

> As a literary event [*Uncle Tom's Cabin*] was the greatest since Prescott's *Ferdinand and Isabella.* . . . It sent Heine back to his Bible and made such an impression on Tolstoy in Russia that, when he came to write *What Is Art?* he took it as an example of the highest type, with Dostoievsky's *House of the Dead* and much of Victor Hugo. Was Tolstoy right in his opinion? On the whole, yes, ten times right. Everything in Mrs. Stowe was large, her experience, her humor, her feeling for justice, her passion for the realities of human nature. Her mind had the swing and rhythm of the great story-tellers like Dickens, Cooper, Scott and Victor Hugo. . . . "A work is great," says Mr. Joad, "when it has ceased to matter that it is bad." Dickens was also great enough to be "bad". . . . Removed from the atmosphere in which it was written, *Uncle Tom's Cabin* remained a great folk-picture of an age and nation.[21]

I quarrel, not with Brooks's estimate, which provides the insights necessary for a critical revaluation, but with his stipulation that the defects of *Uncle Tom's Cabin* should be excused on the ground that it belongs to the category of folk literature.

90

The identification of the careless, powerful art of the popular writer with folk art occurs often in contemporary letters. It is encountered in criticisms of Dreiser and Thomas Wolfe, most frequently in connection with Mark Twain.

> The universal love that Americans have shown for *Huckleberry Finn* is perhaps the best example of the thing regionalist writers strive for. There is so close a bond between material and artist and audience that the book is a folk classic. It is so completely accepted that people do not even think of it as literature.[22]

Mark Twain himself established precedent for removing his work from the "literary" category: "I like history, biography, travel, curious facts and strange happenings, and science, and I detest novels, poetry and theology." And there was much in his personal gifts, his public life, and his literary method to propagate the image of Mark Twain as a folk artist. Yet the deliberate, sophisticated use of folk materials and the vernacular does not make him one. Neither does his popular success. *Huckleberry Finn* is actually more apposite to the problem of the sociological bearings of criticism than *Uncle Tom's Cabin*. Rescued from the limbo to which a genteel criticism once consigned it, *Huckleberry Finn* no longer need be regarded as a special example of popular literature or of folk art, but may be judged by the greatness of its literary performance alone.

Inasmuch as the modern artist employs folk forms, folk methods, and folk materials, whether deliberately or unconsciously, these elements come within the province of criticism. The identification of modern popular literature with folk art, however, is usually framed, not upon the internal properties of popular literature, but upon its social effects, or perhaps upon a preconception of the proper social role of literature. The entire operation is unhistorical: first, in ignoring the function of folk art in primitive society; second, in underestimating the inevitable stratification in modern society of culture in general, literary culture in particular. The operation is also uncritical. It promotes, the already widespread inability to distinguish between genuine and spurious folk art: by deprecating craft, discipline, and convention, it conveys a false impression of the properties of genuine folk art. Finally, by postulating a functional difference between popular and folk art on the one hand and sophisticated art on the other, it sets up a double scale of values. The effect is to withdraw both folk art and popular art from the jurisdiction of literary criticism as we know it.

The danger latent in a relativism according to which "bad" becomes "great" by shifting the perspective from sophisticated to popular is actually realized when nationality, no longer used as a category in criticism, becomes a positive criterion of literary value.

> In days to come, Whittier's poems, the poems of all the Whittier circle, found little favor in critical eyes, even less than the poems of Cambridge. Too many were relics of lapsed occasions, while others seemed as merely pretty as the wild rose, the goldenrod, the laurel; and the wintry winds of the modern mind blew them off the landscape. But the goldenrod rises again in its season, and the folk poem recovers its meaning when the heart of a nation, grown old, returns to its youth. Literature abounds in special sanctions, those that govern national anthems and other expressions of faith,—hymns, folk-poems and ballads,—where the only point that essentially matters is whether the feeling, being true, is also sufficiently large and important. Whittier possessed this immunity.[23]

Whereas Constance Rourke advocates a cultural relativity that permits the retention of critical standards within the integral cultural unit, Brooks reduces the national element in literature to its social (ritual) function, which, however real, cannot be apprehended by criticism.

4

Traditional Society and the New Criticism

THERE WAS a time, a decade or more ago, when regionalism was a more lively issue in American letters than it is today. Its present suspension as a forensic topic may well be a result of intervening events; in a time of war to think in less than national terms became indecorous. Another, perhaps more cogent, explanation is that during the 'forties literary discussion became more technical and less political, in inverse proportion to the violence of politics itself. Though the significance of regionalism as a literary, cultural, and social doctrine exceeded its temporal counterrevolutionary intention, it was most vigorous and articulate when it stood in almost single-handed opposition to the Marxist conquest of American letters. The primary issue in that dispute was neither social nor political, but methodological. Literary or cultural regionalism was a secondary dogma invoked in a political decade to support a critical method that has since become ascendant in the literary scene—the method of the new criticism.

The particular example of regionalism alluded to—Southern agrarianism—is coextensive neither with regionalist thinking as a whole nor with the new criticism itself. The regionalist movement of our time, in both its literary and sociological phases, is much too broad to be identified with any one literary school. It includes nationalist and primitivist critics whose point of view is as far removed as possible from the literary theory of the new critics. On the other hand, the term "new criticism" refers to the work of a fairly heterogeneous group, not

93

all of whom have been directly engaged in the regionalist movement. Nevertheless, in its American manifestation, the new criticism is closely identified with the poet-critics who founded the movement of Southern agrarianism and who have not since renounced their claim to be regionalist writers. Some of these who were later to become so influential as critics began their careers as poets; regional awareness was undoubtedly part of their intuitive experience before it became articulate as theory. They were conscious of belonging to a group and of participating in a movement that was not long in being recognized as a Southern renaissance. Their principal motive was not regional but aesthetic—the formation of a new sensibility—but the homogeneity of the movement was more apparent in its regional than in its aesthetic features. Other regional phenomena had occurred earlier in American letters, but none so powerfully informed by a sense of identity. The regional aspects of the New England renaissance of the nineteenth century were much more obvious to later commentators than to its leading figures (except possibly Thoreau). The self-conscious regionalism of the contemporary Southern writer, on the other hand, was historically predetermined. His region, unlike other parts of the United States, possessed a tradition of political and cultural difference from the national mean and took pride in deviating from the national pattern.

The professed regionalism of the Southern poet-critics is more relevant to their intentions and practice as poets and novelists than to their criticism. The existence of regionalist poetry and fiction is a fact beyond dispute; so also are theories of literature that promulgate regionalist writing; but a regionalist criticism is an anomaly. The creed of these writers has therefore only an oblique relation to their criticism, both as theory and as practice. Their attachment to a particular region is rationally justified by a theory of culture in general, which in turn forms the intellectual background of their criticism without actually figuring in it. The seeming paradox arises from the conjunction of two incompatibles: a doctrine that assigns the highest value to the local, indigenous character of culture; and a criticism that, adjuring historical and environmental relativism, postulates absolute literary standards.

At this point, a distinction must be made between articulate regionalist programs and the actual phenomena of regional culture or regional literature. Insofar as any writer draws upon a specific locale, whether its physical landscape or the life of its less sophisticated inhabitants—and particularly if it happens to be his native scene—his work may be regarded as regional literature. In this sense many of the world's writers have been regional without perceiving the advantage of a regionalist approach. Sometimes this sort of literature, in which the regional element is the unconscious or adventitious accompaniment of an entirely different intention, may be the basis for a conscious regional movement. Local color, the exploitation of regional idiosyncrasies, was proposed in the late nineteenth and early twentieth centuries as a means of creating an authentic national literature in the United States—that is, a literature unmistakably differentiated from British models. Although it sometimes had political affinities with populism and the idea of the "common man," it was not bent on preserving a regional way of life, but remained a literary movement closely allied with prevailing realistic and nationalist literary theories.

I am not concerned here with regionalist literature itself, whether it be an accidental or a deliberate product, but with the contemporary theory of cultural regionalism as it relates to literature. The term "contemporary" is, in a sense, supererogatory, since all theories of culture are modern: they are formulated only after man perceives his culture as an object susceptible of examination and diagnosis; such objectivity does not occur in even the most aberrant members of a flourishing culture, but is

95

fairly common when a culture enters the actual stage of disintegration. In other words, conscious concern with culture is an indicator of dissolution. The sense of the inner contradiction between culture and a theory of culture pervades the social speculations of the Southern critics and probably vitiated their program. According to this concept, the integration of culture is unconscious; it is not achieved by manipulation or planning. Southern agrarianism, like other social doctrines that have engaged the literary intelligence of our time, is explicitly antipathetic both to the quality of modern life and to the existing social order; unlike other social theories, it is skeptical toward social reform as a means of cultural regeneration. In denying the meliorist premises of both liberal democratic and Marxist social theory, the agrarian sociology deliberately severs itself from the main political tradition of the past two centuries or more. In contradistinction to "liberal" or "progressive" views, the agrarians represented their own doctrine as reactionary. Normally "reaction" implies movement in a direction counter to progress; agrarianism was consequently charged with regression. The accusation is not strictly relevant: whereas other regionalist movements apparently advocate reversion to a more primitive social organization, agrarian reaction denotes a state of mind rather than a program of action. The temper of agrarianism, in its literary branch at least, is that of T. S. Eliot's declaration: "We fight rather to keep something alive than in expectation that anything will triumph." Thus, regional culture is to be supported when it actually exists as a natural, spontaneous way of life; it cannot be created by an act of will, that is, by regional planning based upon a preconceived theory of culture.

In the United States the prevalence of the regionalist idea in its various phases—political, economic, social, and cultural—corresponds to both historical and natural facts. As Van Wyck Brooks says of American literature,

The tendency to regionalism was a natural effect of

96

the size of the country. . . . For writers are moved by love, though they often seem to be moved by hatred; and they learn to love the more by loving the less. They come to know the general by knowing the particular, and this particular is often the spot where they are at home with their own instincts; and there were no more American writers, and none more universal than those who were southerners, westerners, New Englanders first. The wisest American visions had been village visions, the visions of Concord, for instance, and the visions of Camden.[1] Although the literary principles of Brooks and those of the Southern regionalist critics are worlds apart—if not antithetical—there is nothing in Brooks's statement to which the Southern critics could not subscribe. Judging from the agreement of otherwise diametrically opposed literary views on this particular point, the organization of American culture on regionalist lines is incontrovertible, and every effort to describe that culture must acknowledge the importance of regional differences.

The intrinsic character of the regional pattern according to which American culture is articulated is readily explained by circumstances, both geographic and historical: first, the size and diversity of the continent; second, the youthfulness of the nation, which explains why our local cultures have not yet been assimilated in a single, homogeneous national culture. Regional sentiment, therefore, is deeply imbedded in American experience. As Merle Curti points out, regional attachments have always accounted for a certain ambivalence in men's loyalty to the nation. "Throughout the Revolution and long afterward John Adams called both Massachusetts and the United States 'my country'. . . . So common was this duality of meaning that both during and after the war, men spoke of state and nation as 'our country' even in the same sentence."[2] The tension between local and national loyalties is reflected on another plane in speculations concerning the proportions and the proper relations of regional and national culture. In nineteenth-century propaganda on behalf of a national literature, colonialism implied the American writer's absorption in local materials as well as his servility toward British standards and opinion. Breadth and inclusiveness, in other words, were the criteria by which a national literature was to be measured. Today the situation is reversed: regional writing is now viewed as constituting the authentic literature of the United States. The proponents of national culture do not deplore the existence of regional cultures; they realize that the nation is enriched by preserving the cultural integrity and autonomy of the regions.

In some respects cultural regionalism can therefore be reconciled with a nationalist point of view. Most contemporary regionalist programs in the United States have owed something, for example, to the Irish nationalist movement. It is sometimes argued that the American regions constitute culture areas roughly analogous to the countries of Europe, so that the national culture can only be conceived pluralistically.

In all of those regions there has grown up a local society, a local cultural pattern, related to the rest of the country but differing in certain important traits. It is upon those local cultures that the modern artistic movement known as cultural regionalism is founded. Intrinsically one is as good material for art as any other; together they make up the literary and artistic picture of the United States.

The basic concept of regionalism as an artistic philosophy is the same as that of nationalism in most other countries. This is not to say that it is motivated by chauvinism or patriotic local pride. It merely means that the artist must express, if he is to express anything at all, the things he knows best, the knowledge that is both of the brain and the blood. He must be emotionally as well as intellectually linked with his materials. He must deal with the patterns of cul-

> ture out of which his own life has grown, and
> through intense interest in the particulars of that
> life attempt to reach the universal expression of
> human character and living. . . . An examination of
> any literature shows that only through his interest
> in the near, the immediate, the familiar does the
> artist reach the fullest communication of his best
> and deepest thoughts.[3]

The philosophy here propounded does not argue the
merits of any one specific regional culture; it encourages
diversity within the national frame and welcomes without prejudice the artistic products of all regions. In perceiving diversity and differentiation as positive values,
liberal or eclectic regionalism extends the original argument for cultural nationalism to regional culture.
Whereas cultural nationalism during the romantic movement was a reaction against cosmopolitan rationalism,
contemporary regionalism strives to preserve the autonomy and identity of local cultures in the face of an
even more powerful leveling force—the uniform culture
of industrial technology. An eclectic regionalism, therefore, does not conflict with cultural nationalism, provided
that the latter also tolerates diversity. National culture
is envisaged as a federation of interacting regional cultures, each enriching the others.

On the level of the ideal, the Southern agrarians enter-
tained a similar conception of regionalism. According to
Donald Davidson, "Regionalism is neither a reversion to
a primitive and simple economy, nor an attempt 'to re-
vive sectionalism under a less offensive name,' but it is a
necessary, organic feature of an advanced and well-
ordered national civilization." Davidson quotes with full
approval a distinction made by Howard Odum: whereas
regionalism "envisages the nation first, making the national culture and welfare the final arbiter," sectionalism
"sees the section first and the nation afterwards." Regionalism implies "component and constituent parts of the
larger national culture," but sectionalism "emphasizes

political boundaries and state sovereignties" and "separateness."[4] The movements of cultural nationalism in Europe have been as much political as linguistic or cultural; but in the United States, speculation about culture tends to make a radical separation between culture and politics, politics being viewed as a secular, anticultural activity. The regionalist's antinational bias becomes apparent in his attitude toward political nationalism. Concerning the corruption of the idea of nationalism, Lewis Mumford writes:

> In the case of a country like America, it led to an attempt to identify as American a particular set of political institutions, which spread over a country of great diversity. Love of country, love of one's folk . . . were both thinned out in order to provide motive power for political and economic combinations that occupied the rulers of the modern state. . . . And so the innocent emotions and feelings which bind men to their village, with its familiar landmarks and familiar faces, were canalized into fuel tanks of emotional suspicion and hatred directed against other nations.[5]

Although the agrarians have no great intellectual affinity with Mumford, particularly in respect to literature, they do share his view that national politics and economy may corrupt the local cultures. Davidson depicts the ideal national culture as a hierarchy of regional cultures, but his attitude toward political and economic actualities precludes the possibility of realizing that ideal in the United States.

The typical literary nationalist in our time situates the generative principle of national culture in the political ideals and institutions of the American people. The agrarians, on the other hand, regard these ideals and institutions as abstractions that, instead of emerging spontaneously from the concrete conditions of American experience, have been superimposed upon them. In their opinion the unity thus produced is factitious, not genuinely related to the diversity of culture and economy throughout the country. Against the modern political state—a rational abstraction—the agrarians counter-poise the regional community—a functional, organic society founded upon a way of life that has emerged gradually in intimate rapport with a specific locale. If such a community is the preliminary condition of culture, it follows that national culture, in the contemporary American context, is spurious. Although the strategy of the Southern agrarians in the 1930's was to endorse all regional cultures, they were concerned chiefly with their own region; they defended the South against aspersions that had been accumulating for several generations and that, although pretending to a national outlook, actually represented only the urban North. The defense of the South served to antagonize non-Southern readers—an effect that may have been intended; but the agrarians' role as apologists for the South obscured their real motive—a philosophic indictment of modern life. Their allegiance to Southern culture was never so profoundly informed as its unstated premise—the conviction of cultural breakdown. It was always understood that the model they proposed was not the contemporary but the old South, about whose cultural shortcomings the most powerful minds of the group had no illusions.

Though the structure of American society dictates the regional basis of culture in the agrarian sociology, neither "regionalism" nor "agrarianism" denotes the philosophical position of the critics associated with the movement. The case for regional differentiation and for the indigenous attributes of literature is made by writers of a different stamp. What distinguishes the Southern critics from those writers is an idea of culture consonant with a radical literary philosophy. The political, sociological, and ultimately philosophical interests of the Southern critics are determined by their experience as contemporary writers and poets. Their conclusions follow from a personal perception of what Allen Tate calls the major premise of T. S. Eliot's thought—the disintegration of of individual consciousness. The intermediate process leading to these conclusions is a historical one—an examination of the conditions that formed the modern consciousness and those that preceded an era of disintegration. The frankly retrospective feature of Southern agrarianism—its brief for an economy based on agriculture—is also differentiated from other agrarian philosophies by its cultural emphasis. The Southern critics are devoted to sophisticated, even to "difficult," art; complexity of structure and meaning stands higher in their scale of values than the spontaneous utterance of emotion. As John Crowe Ransom noted, after Milton it was no longer possible to write folk poetry.

The Southern critics exhibit the generic properties of regionalism and agrarianism mainly in their economics and politics. They are dissatisfied with the obvious features that set modern society off most sharply from previous societies. According to Ransom's declaration of principles, regionalism is opposed to "cosmopolitanism, progressivism, industrialism, free trade, interregionalism, internationalism, eclecticism, liberal education, the federation of the world, or simply rootlessness."[6] This constellation of terms refers primarily to modern culture in its material manifestations—to politics, economics, technology, and education—all of which have been attacked by contemporary social critics on various grounds. The Southern agrarian attack is distinguished by its philosophical groundwork, a metaphysics that denies naturalistic monism, scientific rationalism, positivism—in short, denies the intellectual mode and moral temper of modern life.

Agrarian social criticism is a logical outgrowth of an antipositivist metaphysics in that it assails modern civilization at the point where science has left the most palpable mark on culture: the socioeconomic consequences of industrial technology. Agrarianism recoils from the devastations wrought upon culture by large-scale indus-

102

trialism; in this negative aspect it shares with the contemporary artistic sensibility the widespread repugnance toward the tyranny of the machine. In its positive aspect, agrarianism sometimes involves belief in a direct and even mystical relation between culture and nature, between art and the soil. Davidson's *The Attack on Leviathan,* for example, concludes with a paraphrase of A. E.'s *The Interpreter:*

> The poet Lavelle is ruled by the earth-spirit. Like a true Celtic mystic, he believes in intuitive communion with nature and the gods of nature. He is a nationalist or perhaps he is a regionalist—who holds that the earth-spirit makes for diversity of life. Every race has its own culture, and the races or nations follow "archetypal images." It is a tyranny, or indeed, sacrilege, to violate the resulting unity or "orchestration of race," by imposition from without. ... But I believe that our best wisdom ... arises in the soul and is an emanation from the earth-spirit, a voice speaking directly to us dwellers on the land. ... In countries where they have lost the primeval consciousness of unity with the earth-spirit they have no mythology and cosmogony and thought is materialistic. ...[7]

This quasi-mystical, primitivist strain occurs in most regional and agrarian movements; but it does not figure—nor is it required—in the sociology of either Ransom or Tate, which rationally deduces the virtues of an agrarian economy from the functional relation between a culture and its economy. Culture, as Ransom and Tate understand it, is rooted in a way of life that has existed long enough to produce a coherent tradition. Accordingly, in a genuine culture the economic activities of individuals are integrated with all their other activities. Integration will be more readily achieved in an agrarian society where the individual participates directly in an economic process than in a society where the process can be grasped only as an abstraction. The principle of local and hereditary landownership provides, furthermore, the stability and permanence without which a society can neither create nor transmit culture.

The polarity of agrarianism and industrialism in regionalist doctrine has as its corollary the opposition between "rural" and "urban." The scene of the greatest impact of industrial technology upon society is the metropolis; the development of the modern city is therefore crucial in modern culture. According to the agrarian-regional hypothesis, the culture of the giant city is spurious. Along with the argument for decentralization, the gross size of the culture area is of primary importance in regionalist theory, since population size as well as geographical extent is a limiting factor in cultural integration. Further, metropolitan culture—or nonculture—is held to be the greatest threat to the autonomy and diversity of the regions. "Leviathan" represents, not only the overt tyranny of the national state, but also the indirect tyranny of the metropolis—a standardized, uniform, commercial culture imposed upon the native culture of the regions. Aversion for metropolitan culture, specifically that of New York, is not peculiar to the Southern agrarians, but is common to a broad segment of American thought. Its basis is the fact that metropolitan culture bears no organic relation to native conditions and is mainly of foreign derivation.

A representative exposition of the regionalist-agrarian argument against metropolitan culture is Herbert Agar's essay "Culture and Colonialism." Agar attributes to the metropolis many of the aberrations of the 1920's—cosmopolitanism, bohemianism, expatriation, the contempt for native values, in short, alienation from American culture. Metropolitan culture is decadent; its characteristics are skepticism, despair, nihilism, relativity, and rootlessness. It is derivative rather than native, hence "colonial." The real America is to be discovered in the rural (that is, the regional) community. The intellectual source of Agar's sociology is Spengler's distinction between culture and civilization. Culture represents that high point in the cultural life cycle when the whole configuration is harmoniously formed—when the art, science, politics, and techniques of a culture are completely interlaced and interact mutually. Culture occurs in a social organization distinguished by the fluid relation between the relatively small urban center and the surrounding countryside. The ideal situation exists, therefore, when centralization and diffusion have reached a proper balance. Culture, in Spengler's scheme, is destined to be superseded by the stage of civilization in which the harmonious interplay of cultural functions is destroyed and the values achieved by culture are degraded. The sign of civilization is the world-city as opposed to the culture-city. The world-city creates new social classes incapable of producing culture: the dispossessed urban proletariat and the uprooted urban intelligentsia, both unrelated to the staying traditions of the land, property, and the folk. Spengler's philosophy was fatalistic and pessimistic, aristocratic, and fundamentally anti-intellectual. Being also nationalistic and militaristic, it later fell into disrepute in the circles that had found it so convincing in the 'twenties. But some elements of Spengler's thought have had a perennial attraction for certain American minds: its nostalgia for preindustrial culture; its appeal to authority and tradition rather than to the free play of the intellect, to corporate purpose rather than to individual freedom; and, finally, its fundamental affinity with all other contemporary orthodoxies that oppose the liberal, evolutionary outlook of modern pragmatism and positivism.

Antipathy toward the prevailing intellectual temper of the modern era—which Allen Tate calls positivism and Lewis Mumford, pragmatic liberalism—draws into one orbit a wide variety of critics who are appalled by the spectacle of cultural disintegration and by its effects upon art and sensibility. A fundamental difference, however, between the social views of the Southern critics and those of other traditionalists is revealed in the former's politics. Nearly all American literary critics in the present century who have devoted themselves to social questions have been opposed to capitalism as it evolved in conjunction with large-scale industrialism. The Marxists, of course, had no animus against industrialiasm as such, but only against its political context in the United States. The liberal critics, espousing a more or less doctrinaire socialism sometimes indistinguishable from Marxism, felt that capitalism was no longer compatible with the democratic intentions of the original American political design. They were committed to a program of reform national in scope and founded upon principles of social justice, individual liberty, and equality of political and economic opportunity. None of these motives appears in the Southern agrarian case against capitalism, which, unlike the socialist position, is not based on the issue of private ownership. The agrarians opposed, instead, absentee ownership—that is, finance capitalism. It represents, first, the error of an economy based on remote financial manipulation, unrelated to the practical economic activities of the community. Second, it is the instrument whereby the national state coerces the regions into a standard, uniform economic and cultural pattern. More specifically, it is the means by which the industrial and commercial North is destroying the agrarian South.

The agrarians' economic views, though clearly defined, were not implemented by a political program; and, since politics is a pragmatic activity, agrarianism may be called apolitical. The agrarians denounce national politics on the same grounds as they denounce a uniform national economy. The central feature of agrarian sociology is the distinction it makes between abstract social institutions (such as the modern political state) and communities founded upon a concrete way of life comprising traditional modes of thought, feeling, and behavior. The concept of "community" as constituting the total experience of the members of a society is not far removed from "culture" in its anthropological sense. The social criteria

106

of the agrarians are therefore cultural rather than political or economic. Furthermore, since culture is largely an involuntary and unconscious process, the agrarians doubt the feasibility of major social reforms and of social planning in general; their sociology is thus set off from the main tradition of American social thought based on the idea that man and society are infinitely perfectible. The heterodoxy of agrarianism with respect to official American doctrines is apparent in the corollary of its antidynamic politics—the conception of the fixed status or traditional society, as unequivocally stated by Allen Tate. Such a society is a direct antithesis of liberal democracy, which nominally dispenses with social status, although social stratification continues to exist as a fluid, ambiguous phenomenon. Since the familiar antithesis of democracy is aristocracy, the traditional society is sometimes disparaged as being aristocratic; its proponents assert, however, that it is not properly so, since status in the traditional society derives from function rather than privilege.

In marked contrast with so-called positivist sociologies, agrarian social speculation relinquishes the projection of future societies; the lineaments of the traditional society are necessarily discerned in preindustrial societies. For the Southern critics the pre-Civil War South embodies, however imperfectly, the characteristics of a traditional society. Before 1850, by which time the last vestiges of the theocratic state had been obliterated, New England seemed to preserve some of the same attributes. These American examples, however, only approximate the conditions requisite for an integrated culture. According to the traditionalist analysis, the sources of disintegration antedate by some centuries the several revolutions, political and technological, that have shaped the modern era. The revolutions, however, are symptoms rather than causes. The intellectual and spiritual origins of disintegration are to be sought in the era that inaugurated the modern consciousness—the European Renaissance. The most nearly perfect instance of a traditional society is the Christian society of Dante's Europe or perhaps the twelfth-century society celebrated by Henry Adams. The antisecular aspects of agrarian sociology are sometimes ascribed (inaccurately, it would seem) to sentimental nostalgia for the Middle Ages. Actually, the "mediaeval synthesis" serves as a fixed point of reference, a standard by which to judge the degrees of disintegration in subsequent societies.

The political and economic aspects of the traditional society are complementary; they are deduced from the conditions deemed favorable for that stability and permanence without which a society may neither receive nor transmit culture. The agrarian sociology posits a functional economics founded on hereditary landownership—a hierarchical, "graded" society in which status is mainly, though not entirely, inherited. A distinguishing feature, according to Allen Tate, for whom "feudal" designates such a society, is a native peasantry bound to the land. "All great cultures have been rooted in peasantries, in free peasantries."[8] These political-economic conditions constitute the social framework that alone can support and foster a genuine culture, though they do not in themselves indicate its nature.

The prime desideratum of culture, as may be inferred from the agrarian criticism of modern life, is integration. The hypothesis of cultural integration is by now a staple of sociological discourse; the traditionalist sociology, however, is distinguished by its emphasis on religion as the indispensable binding element. The virtue of the traditional society, accordingly, inheres in the moral and intellectual qualities conferred upon it by a central religious authority. It possesses, as modern liberal society does not, "a coherent way of thinking about experience, a unified conception of man in relation to God and nature."[9] The culture of such a society provides the individual with "an external framework of ideas," an objective system of truth and value. Culture thus becomes interchangeable with traditions; a tradition, according to Allen Tate, is "formed of a structure of absolutes, imperatives or points of moral and intellectual reference which man requires to realize his nature." The collapse of the universal Catholic order of the Middle Ages, the decay of the hierarchical social structure, deprived modern man of the means for ordering and judging experience. The end product of this long process is the spiritual and intellectual disorder of our age.

The most thorough exponent of an antisecular sociology in our time is T. S. Eliot, who is neither a Southern regionalist nor an agrarian, although sympathetic to both movements. Judging from the social as well as the literary affinity between Eliot and the Southern poet-critics, there may be more than a fortuitous relation between the literary theory of the new criticism and the social and cultural views articulated by certain of the new critics. These are the views of men interested primarily in literature and—at least by Eliot's own admission—only secondarily in society. The question is not whether their social convictions are determined by their literary opinions (or vice versa), but to what extent the relation between these two elements of their thought is integral. The nature of the relation is obscured by their apparent reluctance to discuss literary and sociocultural matters in the same text. The essays of Ransom, Tate, and Davidson on political and social topics, which appeared in the 'thirties, are distinct from their literary essays; nor is Eliot's *Notes towards a Definition of Culture* explicitly concerned with the status of literature and the arts in general culture. The tendency on the part of these writers to separate social speculation from literary discourse is undoubtedly induced by knowledge of the extraordinary complexity of literature as an art as well as by mistrust of a facile determinism that merely reduces literary properties to their social or ideological components.

Current misunderstanding of the theoretical principles of the new criticism arises from failure to discriminate between its idea of literature as a cultural product and its idea of the function and limits of criticism. In proscribing the relevance of historical information to literary judgment, the new criticism neither asserts that literature has no history nor denies that it exists in a cultural context. The method of the new criticism originated as a reaction, not against historical scholarship, but against the excesses of historical, sociological, and psychological criticism. Since these critical modes all center upon the "extrinsic" relations of the literary work, they tended to dissolve the work into a complex of relations and forces that, though anterior to it, do not reside in the work itself. In opposing this tendency, the new critics undoubtedly miscalculated the ability of criticism to dispense with historical information. Furthermore, their severe textual approach and concentration upon the internal structure of the poem were erroneously interpreted as signifying that literature exists in a historical vacuum. These methods were designed to apprehend the integrity of the individual work, a concrete and finite object, and incidentally to preserve that integrity from the abstracting effects of reductive criticism. Though the work is culturally determined, it differs from other cultural products in that its value is not derivative but actually inheres in its singularity. In theory this position denies the relevance, in critical judgment, of the instrumental functions of literature, communicative or affective; it centers upon the autonomous or "ontological" properties of individual works. In contrast with neoclassic critical doctrine, which presumes the primary function of literature to be moral instruction, and romantic doctrine, which presumes it to be expression, the new criticism regards these functions as accidental rather than definitive; the nature of the literary work is defined by aesthetic properties. It would be convenient to label the new criticism "aesthetic" criticism except for the ambiguity of the term "aesthetic" as applied to literary art. The new critics subscribe to the fundamental doctrine that the distinguishing element in literature is aesthetic, but they do not agree on the validity of critical judgment based exclusively on aesthetic criteria. Ransom, for instance, proposes a more severely aesthetic standard than Tate, whereas Eliot has gone further than most "aesthetic" critics in advocating extra-aesthetic criteria.

The argument that information about the genesis of a particular work is irrelevant to its existence as an aesthetic, autonomous whole does not rule out the hypothesis of cultural determination; nor does it enjoin speculation on this topic apart from the critical act. But the aesthetic critic is wary of simple formulas representing the relation between art and society. Since aesthetic quality may not be inferred from social and cultural conditions and since critical judgment may refer only to particular works, the aesthetic critic does not assume with the historical critic that artistic decadence results directly and inevitably from social disintegration. Nevertheless, the aesthetic critic allows that artistic activity, as an integral part of culture, is impaired in a disintegrated society. Within this limited area social and cultural questions are entirely apposite to literary questions.

The conception of aesthetic autonomy is postulated, like the idea of the traditional society, upon the conviction that science or (to use Tate's term) positivism is not the only possible mode of cognition; aesthetic perception is itself considered to be a cognitive act providing knowledge of a kind distinct from the scientific. Aesthetic cognition is qualitative; science is quantitative. The latter abstracts evidence from phenomena for specific purposes; the former apprehends the entire discrete phenomenon for its own sake. Whereas science is an instrument of the practical will, the aesthetic whole resists practical formulation. The ulterior uses to which a work of art may be put are ancillary to its mode of existence as an object of contemplation.

According to the new critics, the modern world, dedicated to positivism and pragmatic values, fosters neither aesthetic sensibility nor aesthetic experience; the culture of urban industrial society actually suppresses them. In the traditional or religious society, where reason and faith are distinct yet mutually interactive categories, aesthetic vision occurs as naturally as spiritual vision. The direct relation between a traditional society and aesthetic experience is most explicitly stated in Ransom's essay "Forms and Citizens." Ransom assumes in human behavior a dualism that may be expressed as "natural" as against "social" behavior. The natural man is "a predatory creature to whom every object is an object of prey and the real or individual object cannot occur"; the social man "submits to the restraint of convention, comes to respect the object and to see it unfold at last its individuality." Parallel with these is the dualism of economic forms and aesthetic forms, of utility and gratuitous experience. The proper aim of society is to repress or at least to channel the instinctive, "natural" impulses by imposing upon them a "humanist" order.

Societies of the old order seemed better aware of the extent of their responsibilities. Along with the work-forms went the play-forms, which were elaborate in detail, and great in number, fastening upon so many of the common and otherwise practical occasions of life and making them occasions of joy and reflection, even festivals and celebrations; yet at the same time by no means a help but if anything a hindrance to direct action. The aesthetic forms are a technique of restraint, not of efficiency. They do not butter our bread, and they delay the eating of it. They stand between the individual and his natural object and impose a check upon his action. . . . To the concept of direct action the old society—the directed and hierarchical one—opposed the concept of aesthetic experience, as a true opposite, and checked the one in order to induce the other.[10]

112

If aesthetic experience was normal in traditional so-cieties, it might be inferred that the artist's situation then was happier than it is now; both his aesthetic aims and his social status were more certain, since he could count on a wide, receptive audience. Ransom does not stipulate the nature or quality of the art produced in the traditional society; for that matter, he does not specifi-cally discuss art in this essay. Yet his thesis—"the object of a proper society is to instruct its members how to transform instinctive experience into aesthetic experi-ence"—indicates how closely the idea of the traditional society conforms to the conception of art as autonomous. The transformation is accomplished by imposing form and order upon unreflective experience, just as the work of art itself is a formal ordering of experience.

Central in the literary doctrine of the new criticism is form, the quality or attribute that constitutes the aes-thetic character of a work. The new criticism is therefore often called "formalist." This designation is no more accurate than "aesthetic," being usually taken to signify indifference to content. The idea of the separability of form and content actually violates the concept of aes-thetic integrity, according to which no element in a work may be abstracted from the whole or established as its essence. Form, properly considered, is the discipline by means of which life or experience is transmuted into art; the transmutation, having been made, is no longer sus-ceptible of analysis: form and content are now organi-cally fused.

It is hardly necessary, however, to press the analogy between the work of art and the traditional society as formal, integrated, organic wholes in order to perceive the relation between social and literary ideas in the Southern critics. The relation is founded upon more cogent grounds—their experience as poets rather than as critics. In them the impulse leading from poetry to social theory arises from personal awareness of the poet's predicament in modern society—the difficulty of pro-

113

ducing a formal poetry in an era of disintegration. Initially felt as personal, the poet's situation was recognized as a cultural, hence social, problem. It is, of course, impossible to discuss the poetic experience of these men except as it is reflected in their criticism. One feature of this criticism is a radical opposition toward romantic poetry and theory. The fallacy of romantic poetic practice, according to the new critics, stems from the assumption that art can be created independently of poetic culture. The point of view was stated definitively in Eliot's "Tradition and the Individual Talent," which discredited the notion of poetry as a spontaneous expression of personal emotion and which reaffirmed poetic culture—the poetic tradition of the Western world—as indispensable to the poet's discipline. The romantic doctrine is more explicitly described by Yvor Winters as the fallacy of "imitative form"—the notion that the poet achieves form by expressing his consciousness or by imitating nonordered or disordered experience. According to the contrary view, poetry requires a rational structure consciously controlled by the poet; control is a matter, not of individual discovery, but of a living tradition.

In this context "tradition" refers to literary tradition, and "culture" to literary culture. But as already shown, the term "tradition" in the social discourse of the Southern critics is much broader in scope, much more complex. The transition from the narrower to the broader concept is best explained in connection with the concept of poetic form. According to Allen Tate, the modern poet is baffled by the loss of a scheme of objective reference, which alone could confer order and meaning upon his emotional experience; hence the failure of poetic talent in our time to integrate sensation and consciousness in aesthetic form. The formal ordering of experience that constitutes poetry obviously signifies more than the use of the formal and technical devices transmitted by the tradition of a craft or discipline. A poetic tradition,

114

though indispensable, is inadequate for creating form in poetry unless it is also integrated with a cultural tradition. In the latter context tradition, according to Tate, is a "quality of judgment and conduct, rooted in a concrete way of life that we inherit from our immediate past. . . . Tradition . . . no less than religion, is formed of a structure of absolutes, imperatives, or points of intellectual and moral reference which man requires to realize his nature."[11]

It now becomes clear that the formal rendering of experience that is poetry cannot be entirely willed by the individual poet; poetic ability is determined, at least in part, by the culture of the poet's society.

> What is the nature of a poet's culture? Or, to put the question properly, what is the meaning of culture for poetry? . . . Learning has never had anything to do with culture except instrumentally: the poet must be exactly literate enough to write down fully and explicitly what he has to say, but no more. The source of a poet's true culture lies back of the paraphernalia of culture, and not all the strenuous activity of this enlightened age can create it.
>
> A culture cannot be consciously created. It is an available source of ideas that are imbedded in a complete and homogeneous society. . . . The prior conditions for great poetry, given a great talent, are just two: the thoroughness of the poet's discipline in an objective system of truth, and his lack of consciousness of such a discipline. For this discipline is a number of fundamental ideas the origin of which the poet does not know; they give form and stability to his fresh perceptions of the world; and he cannot shake them off. This is his culture.[12]

The poet's relation to his culture may be viewed in two distinct, but not exclusive, perspectives—sociological and aesthetic. The nature of culture determines his relation to his audience; hence his status and dignity in society. Even though great poetry has rarely been a

115

popular art in highly integrated societies, the modern poet's situation has deteriorated to an unprecedented degree; he has been deprived, not only of a fluent relation with his entire society, but also of the segment of it that formerly constituted a dependable audience. The traditionalist critic offers the explanation for this breakdown: there is no longer a central and common agreement about the value and meaning of existence, nor a common convention of language and symbol in which agreement is contained. The reconstitution of the artist's social role is an implied, if not an explicit, motive of the traditional sociology. The chief argument for a society integrated on the organic principle is that all its constituent activities function harmoniously, complementing and fulfilling each other. In such a society aesthetic activity is promoted by practical activity, not stifled by it.

Some have accused the traditionalist critics of preferring former societies on aesthetic rather than humanitarian grounds. But this charge, by implying a direct correspondence between the nature of society and the nature of art, imputes to the traditionalist critic a more thoroughgoing determinism than he is willing to accept. According to Tate, the conditions of culture, over which the poet has no control and of which he must be largely unaware, determine the quality of his work. The relation of poetry to culture and society is problematical; Tate, for example, believes that the conditions in which society and culture flourish may not necessarily favor poetry. The propitious moment for great poetry does not coincide, it seems, with the fullest realization of cultural stability and homogeneity, but actually occurs when a tradition has nearly spent itself. In other words, poetry has a negative as well as a positive relation to society. The condition necessary for great poetry is a tension between individual consciousness and an inherited cultural tradition. It is formed by the impact of a highly personal, concrete, immediate perception upon an existing, unconscious moral and intellectual world view.

116

Personal revelation of the kind that Donne and Miss Dickinson strove for, in their effort to understand their relation to the world, is a feature of all great poetry; it is probably the hidden motive for writing. It is the effort of the individual to live apart from a cultural tradition that no longer sustains him. But this culture is ... indispensable: there is a good deal of shallow nonsense in modern criticism which holds that poetry—and this is a half truth that is worse than false—is essentially revolutionary. It is only indirectly revolutionary: the intellectual and religious background of an age no longer contains the whole spirit, and the poet proceeds to examine the background in terms of immediate experience. But the background is absolutely necessary; otherwise all the arts, not only poetry, would have to rise in a vacuum. Poetry does not dispense with tradition; it probes the deficiencies of a tradition. But it must have a tradition to probe.[13]

It is thus apparent that great poetry—poetry that charges sensation with the greatest possible amount of thought and emotion—is not the product of society at its happiest; for at that point the poet is incapable of opposing personal vision to the prevailing intellectual and moral structure. Great poetry is had at the price of social disintegration. But it should not thereby be assumed that modern society nurtures the production of a great poetry. For when disintegration is far advanced and a coherent cultural tradition has disappeared, the poet is compelled to overstrain the resources of individual sensibility, as Hart Crane did; or to resurrect an archaic tradition; or to create an arbitrary convention, as Yeats did, by an act of will—all of which procedures have been too great a burden for the poetic talent of our time.

5

The Transatlantic Element

FROM THE MOMENT American literary opinion began to regard our literature as an independent entity, it confronted the problem of correlating American with European literature, and particularly with English literature. For nearly a century American writers had oscillated between optimism and pessimism on the score of literary independence. On the one hand, the separateness and worth of native letters were declared in innumerable essays, orations, and manifestos, most of which betrayed in their hortatory tone a certain defensiveness; on the other hand, the subordinate status of American letters was accepted with resignation and even with a sort of inverted pride. Beginning at some point in the present century (for convenience, I assume 1914 as the date), there was a concerted effort to reaffirm the identity of American literature. In order to endow belief in that identity with conviction and substance, the earlier literature was rediscovered and revaluated and contemporary writing was vindicated. Today no one doubts seriously either the identity or the importance of American literature; but so long as the doubt survived, it impeded a mature criticism.

The uncertainties of a whole century were not, however, automatically dispelled by the new attitude, nor are they likely to disappear from the atmosphere of literary discussion. Notwithstanding wide acceptance of the nationalist thesis, contemporary criticism is deeply schismed, revealing far-reaching differences about the status of American in comparison with other literatures and with literature in general. Our present confidence in the identity of American letters has only intensified the ambivalence toward Europe that exists at the center of nearly all vital controversies in American criticism. Obviously more is here involved than the relation to European literature. This relation is included in a broader, more stubborn question—the relation between cultures. Inasmuch as the critic is an American, his own attitudes, are affected by that permanent ambivalence toward Europe in American thought—an ambivalence that, incidentally, has never been more important than today, when the hegemony of European civilization is being yielded to the United States. No nation hitherto has achieved world power with so much confidence in its capacities and yet with so little self-knowledge of its cultural being.

Our confusion arises partly from the distinction between culture and civilization—a distinction that was never clear and that now appears to be vanishing. In one formulation, still widely accepted, civilization represents the material achievements of a society; culture, the artistic, intellectual, and spiritual achievements. Whatever inferiority Americans have felt refers to European "culture" rather than to European "civilization," for we have rarely doubted that our standard of living and our technology represent a positive advance over Europe. Nor does the sense of cultural inferiority include politics: a fundamental American tenet is belief in the moral superiority of our political institutions. Yet the mixture of attraction and repulsion that characterizes our attitudes toward Europe may well be political in origin.

Actually our political culture was no more indigenous than any other phase of our culture, having been deeply indebted to European political thought, both English and Continental. And yet, during the first years of the republic, there occurred a sharp division between the pro-European and anti-European point of view—a division that has not thus far been completely resolved. According to V. L. Parrington,

The change which came over political thought in

America in consequence of the rise in French Jacobin philosophy is not inadequately revealed in the writings of two men ... Thomas Paine and Thomas Jefferson. Both were speculative thinkers, profoundly in sympathy with French revolutionary ideals; but the former was detached from local patriotisms and national interests, a delegate at large in the cause of human rights.... The latter remained wholly American.... He was primarily concerned to discover principles that would apply to native conditions and further the cause of American democracy.[1]

Jefferson's point of view was to become dominant but not absolute, because the international ideal has always had great intellectual prestige in American political thought.

Our defensive attitude toward Europe and European culture was a natural result of our revolutionary origins. Normally defensiveness might have evaporated or survived as a ritual gesture devoid of content. But for nearly a century and a half the revolutionary situation was recreated by each influx of Europeans, who not only repudiated what they had left behind but pinned all their hopes on the properties that differentiated their new home most sharply from Europe. Whereas the descendants of the original revolutionaries would willingly have been reconciled with the old culture, the new arrivals were constantly severing bonds of attachment. Our attitude has been, therefore, compounded perennially of attraction and repulsion, generosity and suspicion; as Constance Rourke observed of American art, "Our relation to Europe is a subject we have never been able to let alone. We have been obsessed by it, and we haven't known what to do about it."[2]

The terms in which the relation is habitually couched—mother country, parent country, the bond or cord between the New World and the Old—are no doubt revealing. The familial metaphor is applied to the facts: America's initial dependence upon European culture;

political severance from Europe and the emergence of a distinct culture; the continuing accretion of European elements in American culture after the achievement of political maturity. Not unnaturally, therefore, responses to the situation are phrased in Freudian terms: acceptance and rejection, inferiority and compensatory aggression, sublimation and ambivalence.

The reception of the Freudian doctrine in the United States illustrates, incidentally, the complexity of American-European cultural relations in our own time. (This statement refers, of course, not to the doctrine's professional reputation, but to its literary and journalistic career.) Freud's ideas were introduced into the literary atmosphere by such writers as Ludwig Lewisohn, Floyd Dell, and Max Eastman. In the 1920's Freud became a cult among those literary figures who were most deeply alienated from American culture and most powerfully drawn toward Europe. At a time when the shortcomings of the native culture were commonly attributed to a repressive puritanism, Freudian doctrine seemed to provide a rationale of the writer's alienation from the national life and to corroborate his attachment to European culture. Enthusiasm for Freud's ideas, often uncritical and superficial, was matched at this time by an equally uncritical mistrust of the new psychology as a corrupt doctrine—the product of European decadence and therefore inapplicable to American conditions. Despite this resistance, rudimentary notions of depth psychology have gradually filtered into the general consciousness of Americans. Today psychoanalysis, though by no means universally accepted, is naturalized to the extent that criticism need no longer take into account its "foreign" origin. The original hostility probably survives, however, as an element in popular suspicion and ridicule of analysis.

Thus the alternating pattern of aggressiveness and submissiveness in the American's attitude toward Europe is a product of political and social history on the one hand, cultural history on the other. Although generalizations on so complex a topic must be oversimple, the aggressive strain would seem to spring from the revolutionary attitude which was continuously revived for well over a century, whereas the submissive strain can be traced to the pre-Revolutionary (colonial) status of American culture. Throughout the nineteenth century it was assumed that the new nation would eventually produce a culture commensurate with the moral superiority of its political institutions and the magnitude of its material achievements. So long as culture was measured by European models, fulfillment was bound to fall short of expectation. Extremes of expectation and of disappointment gave rise to a still-extant polarization of opinion. European culture was simultaneously worshipped and reviled; it was measured both favorably and unfavorably against the crude vigor of American experience.

One effect of these sharp divisions in our sentiment about Europe was to establish a factitious dichotomy of "culture" and "experience." Until a generation or two ago the comparison of American and European culture was generally restricted to intellectual and aesthetic matters. The term "culture" denoted "enlightenment and refinement of taste acquired by intellectual and aesthetic training"; it had not yet acquired the additional sense of "civilization." As used today, the term is hopelessly ambiguous: in literary discourse it may stand for either the narrowest or the broadest denotation; that is, for literary and artistic culture, or for the anthropological usage according to which "culture" denotes a people's whole way of life. But whether it is narrowly or broadly employed, the word is likely to be informed by the insight provided by nineteenth-century history and corroborated by contemporary anthropology—that the elements of culture are interdependent and integrally related. The sharp distinctions formerly made between American literary and artistic culture and American civilization are blurred; it

122

no longer seems feasible to compare American and European culture in any narrow sense.

The hypothesis of cultural integration is undoubtedly among the most fertile modern conceptions. It has been applied with the most striking success in recent anthropological theory. But its value for the study of modern complex cultures and their most highly developed intellectual and aesthetic activities is problematical. Modern literary history, of course, is founded on the idea that literature is integrated with the other activities of a culture. In the first systematic enunciation of the idea by German romantic philosophy, the cultural unit was assumed to be the national state; the principle of integration, the national character. In the ensuing century and a half, literary history developed in a fairly straight line. During the nineteenth century it borrowed information and methods from the social sciences, notably the idea of sociological determinism; but in general the concept of the nation as the normal cultural unit remained intact.

Almost inevitably the effort to view American literary works as a coherent phenomenon borrowed the methods and criteria of European literary history. Nearly all comprehensive accounts of American literature, all assertions of its identity, are founded on the conception of a national culture distinct in kind from anything European. So long as such an assumption allows for the immense complexity of modern cultures and the multiplicity of their literary activities, it need not be challenged. The fallacy latent in the hypothesis of unity and identity is the lure of simplicity and homogeneity—the attraction of the single formula to explain both the national configuration and the national literature. The concept of national character is such a formula. In psychological terms, it indicates the central core of personality common to the members of a national group and transmitted either biologically or by the group culture. Obviously this core must possess a certain plasticity. But the crucial question is, how much aberration can it tolerate before

123

losing its integrity? That depends on the individual's confidence in both its integrity and its permanence. These considerations are also pertinent to the question of national culture. How much diversity can a culture contain before its identity is threatened?

The singularities of our national culture are evident in its historical circumstances. Compared with European national cultures, it has existed only a short time; it was a composite almost from the start, and its multiplicity increased as it developed; the elements of culture, if not the configuration, were derivative, and their origin is a matter of historical knowledge. In the configuration itself, borrowed elements have presumably been fused with an original native situation and subtly modified by it. The precariousness of the balance thus established between foreign and native is evident in the concern of nationalist critics to preserve the balance.

Literary nationalism is not, of course, peculiar to American criticism. It has flourished in Europe for a century and a half, sometimes in conjunction with revolutionary and separatist movements, sometimes with conservative political and religious movements as a conscious reaction against cosmopolitan intellectualism. Literary nationalism in a culture possessing an ancient and well-defined tradition has a different role than in the United States, where the foreign elements do not merely lie on the surface but are deeply ingrained in the culture. The difference is apparent in the sensitiveness of the American literary nationalist to evidence of infidelity. Since the margin between the national and the alien is narrower in America than elsewhere, the nationalist critic is zealous to preserve that margin and is fearful of its being attenuated by further importations. But both his zeal and his fear betray lack of confidence in the reality and the nature of the national configuration. "Despite all bluster, the newly created national ego is at bottom uncertain of its identity; hence the compensatory self-assertion and inability to tolerate even the suspicion of divided loyalties."[3]

Doubt concerning the national identity results partly from our imperfect understanding of modern culture (its nature and composition) and of the intricate process whereby cultures are transported and transmitted and preserved by individuals. Obviously, however, modern cultures are not wholly autochthonous, and cultural integration signifies the integration of disparate elements. The only dissenter to this view is the primitivist who regards culture as an unconscious and primordial element in personality.

> The European cultures, swept to America, and there buried, were half-killed by the mere uprooting. They were never American; they could never live in America. . . . Everywhere the cultures which we call Indian . . . were of a spiritual nature. . . . And everywhere these cultures were buried by the Caucasian floods.[4]

The more moderate view maintains that European cultures were successfully transplanted to America and that from them there emerged a new, distinct culture.

> Bodies of exact knowledge, patterns of thought, and all the agencies of intellectual life developed in America in relation to their counterparts in Europe. Each generation of Europeans who came to America brought prevailing or dissenting European ideas, brought in greater or less knowledge, brought concepts of the good and the beautiful. All these played essential roles in the growth of American thought. . . . Because the American environment, physical and social, differed from that of Europe, Americans confronted by different needs and problems, adopted the European intellectual heritage in their own way. And because American life came increasingly to differ from European life, American agencies of intellectual life, and the use made of

knowledge likewise came to differ in America from their European counterpart.[5]

This description of cultural transit and adaptation emphasizes the pliability of American national culture; it sets no arbitary limit on the capacity of American culture to absorb foreign materials beyond which its identity is endangered. For the identity of a culture is perceived to be the configuration, which may be deduced from the "needs" imposed by a distinctive physical and social setting. Presumably the native configuration acts as a solvent powerful enough to convert alien intellectual elements to native uses. Applied to the study of American literature, this concept should dispel needless fears that the native values may be dissipated in foreign engrossments. The successful transformation of colonial culture plus the subsequent accretions from Europe into a unique American culture might be expected to dispel the critic's fear of "adulteration."

But in practice, cultural nationalism is likely to display a dual response to Europe: gratitude for past contributions, hostility toward present infringement. The duality is illustrated by two passages in Howard Mumford Jones's *Ideas in America*. The first passage protests against a tendency in American criticism to limit the native genius to one segment of American experience; it reaffirms the affinities of American and European culture.

> Turner's classic essay was necessary in its time, but when one finds enthusiasts discovering a frontier element in the novels of Henry James, it is time to remember . . . that the United States is a part of the west-European cultural hegemony, and that its civilization results from the interplay of American *and* European forces. . . . Even in the celebrated instance of the frontier, the concept as it has been worked out by American historians, is open to the constant correction implied in the truth that America is the European frontier through long periods—something Emerson was shrewd enough

to observe when he said that Europe extends to the Alleghanies.[6]
Whereas a broad and liberal conception of American culture is here invoked to conteract the claims of a narrow regionalist outlook, the broad view is apparently abandoned in favor of a conservative one in the second passage, which occurs in an address denouncing contemporary letters and advocating a return to earlier American values, specifically to the tradition of liberal democracy based upon reason and justice.

I offer the suggestion that a principal cause of our lost innocence has been the careless acceptance of powerful European influences without at the same time making the necessary adjustment of these forces to what seems to me to be the American tradition about the function of literature in the Republic. What have these influences been? They have principally been the influence of European realism and naturalism; the influence of Freud; the influence of European politico-social theories, an example being Marxianism; the influence of European invention in technique, from free verse to the fictional method of James Joyce; and the influence of intellectualist criticism, most familiar in the work of such expatriate Americans as Mr. Ezra Pound and Mr. T. S. Eliot. . . . The error of the strange European conquest of American literature which is characteristic of the last twenty-five years is not at once apparent for the reason that it has been paradoxically disguised as a realistic approach to the actualities of the American scene.[7]

Taken together, the two statements of Howard Mumford Jones seem to signify that whereas borrowing was salutary for the infant culture of the nineteenth century, the native tradition, once established, requires protection from foreign ideas and habits. The reversal of attitude toward Europe seems to be based on a time scale. Inasmuch as the terms "tradition" and "culture" are interchangeable, the time element is wholly relevant to culture; obviously a distinctive native culture is not achieved instantaneously, but requires a period of stability in which to crystalize. During this period, conceivably, the emergent tradition may be overwhelmed by sudden invasion. But since the formation of tradition in a young country is aided by time, American culture should, hypothetically, be better armed against invasion now than a century ago.

The conservatism of the literary nationalist is valid inasmuch as it respects the traditional basis of culture; but the attempt to arrest cultural growth at any fixed stage, present or past, ignores the normal process of cultural interchange in the modern world. (Such interchange is not without risks, but the alternative is a censorship imposed by the state.) The uneasiness of the cultural nationalist viewing the complexity of modern culture is revealed in his pastoralism—not so intense as that of the authentic primitivist, yet nonetheless regressive. Modern cultural nationalism, which was created by the counterrevolutionary impulse of the European romantic movement, is nostalgic for simplicity, for the homogeneous societies of the past. The American nationalist critics find simplicity in pre-Civil War America—the agrarian democracy of Jefferson, the New England flowering in the 'forties, or the frontier West.

The simpler image is always more attractive than the complex one, which, viewed at close quarters, appears amorphous. Though the complexity of culture has been increasing at a geometric rate, cultural homogeneity, even in the simplest societies, is relative. The illusion of homogeneity may be merely an effect of historical perspective. The configurational hypothesis provides a valuable method for perceiving unity in diversity without sacrificing awareness of cultural phenomena. The literary nationalist, however, tends to affirm the configuration and deny the culture. Simplicity may be a virtue in both societies and works of art; simplification is an aid to historical technique. But the historical method is sometimes incompatible with the requirements of literary criticism, which deals with infinitely complex cultural phenomena. Any theory of American literature that employs conformity to a unitary national tradition as a standard judgment distorts the idea of literature as a cultural product. It must be remembered that American literature is a wholly modern phenomenon; it was born into a civilization already advanced and composite, equipped with a complex literary tradition derived from centuries of European practice.

The impulse to force American writing into a simple mold, to view it as either faithful or unfaithful to the national character, generally reveals, not only a predilection for a simpler society, but also a romantic view of the relation between literature and society. In literary theory that relation is an equivocal topic; most hypotheses, however, locate the specific characteristic of literary production in the tension created between an individual's perception of life or reality and the writer's total milieu. Dispute centers, first, upon the extent to which the milieu determines the work; second, upon the proportion of individual and cultural ingredients in the work and their relative importance. Romantic literary doctrine emphasizes the primacy of individual perception. As Santayana states it,

> The great merit of the romantic attitude in poetry and of the transcendental method in philosophy, is that they put us back at the beginning of our experience. They disintegrate convention, which is often cumbrous and confused, and restore us to ourselves, to immediate perception and primordial will. . . . This obvious truth would not need to be insisted on but for two reasons: one that conventional knowledge such as our notions of science and morality afford, is often top-heavy: asserts and imposes on us much more than our experience warrants—our experience which is our only approach to reality.

129

The other reason is the reverse or counterpart of this; for conventional knowledge often ignores and seems to suppress parts of experience no less actual and important for us than those parts on which conventional knowledge itself is reared. The public world is too narrow for the soul. . . . It follows that one who has no sympathy with such a philosophy is a comparatively conventional person. He has a second-hand mind. . . . It follows also, however, that one who has no philosophy but this has no wisdom. . . .[8]

Romantic emphasis on originality of perception has been discounted by deterministic literary theory and by modern notions of the comprehensive effect of culture upon personality. The literary nationalist discards the individualistic aspect of the romantic doctrine: after all, his main point is the formative effect of communal experience upon literary production. But he preserves the romantic dichotomy of convention and experience; he incorporates it in his idea of national culture by setting up an opposition between the derivative elements in culture—its learned responses—and the national experience itself. A real distinction exists between culture and experience—culture being transmitted from one generation to the next, whereas experience is not. The two can hardly, however, be construed as opposites, since experience modifies culture but is also mainly determined by it. Recorded experience, being transmissible, becomes culture.

Actually the dichotomy of culture and experience is nothing more than a selection from culture as a whole. The nationalist attributes greater value to the process whereby culture is modified by experience (that is, by the native environment, social and physical) than to the traditional elements in culture. A "national tradition" is a segment of a larger tradition. The separation of culture and experience results in a preoccupation with the differences between the European and the native elements in American culture—the establishment of a scale in which the differences are weighed.

Despite the higher value placed on the native, the literary nationalist normally regards native and European elements as complementary rather than antithetical; he does not proscribe alien elements that have already been firmly incorporated. Carried to its logical extreme, however, romantic antitraditionalism, by crediting environment alone with the capacity to create culture, repudiates all alien elements. D. H. Lawrence, for example, advised American writers to sever all ties with Europe.

> Alas for a people when its tradition is established, and its limit of beauty defined.... What a young race wants is not a tradition nor a bunch of culture monuments. It wants an inspiration.... You must first have faith, faith in your own unrevealed, unknown destiny.... The future is a strange, urgent, poignant responsibility, something which urges inside a young race like sap, or like pregnancy, urging towards fulfillment.... Let Americans turn to America, and to that very America which has been rejected and almost annihilated. Do they want to draw sustenance for the future? They will never draw it from the lovely monuments of our European past. These have an almost fatal narcotic, dream-luxurious effect upon the soul. America must turn again to catch the spirit of her own dark, aboriginal continent.... Americans must again take up life where the Red Indian, the Aztec, the Maya, the Incas left off. They must pick up the life-thread where the mysterious Red race let it fall. They must catch the pulse of life which Cortes and Columbus murdered.

The first part of Lawrence's exhortation recalls Emerson's *American Scholar* and innumerable later appeals for a genuine national literature. But few literary men actually pursue, as Lawrence does, the concept of an indigenous literature to its logical limit—the point at which literature is severed from both history and culture. Lawrence was, of course, no more interested in literary nationalism than in culture; he was imagining a literature as nearly instinctive and nonintellectual as possible.

The extreme instance of primitivism cited here illustrates a propensity of nativist literary theory. Primitivism is a counterpart of the romantic conviction that literature can be created by perception unmediated by traditional forms of knowledge. According to this view, the American writer has one special advantage—the newness of our culture; the native writer, freed from the pressure of convention, responds spontaneously to his environment. The advantage of a new culture is emphasized by contrast with Europe, which is represented as overgrown with dead tradition, hence static and decadent.

A highly original version of the environmentalist thesis is expounded in Ferner Nuhn's *The Wind Blew from the East*, a study of Henry James, Henry Adams, and T. S. Eliot.

> We are peculiarly the children of world space, both by division and extension. The Atlantic Ocean marks the division. A three-thousand-mile continent measures the extension. Our life of course is in space and time together. . . . But we have had an unusual concern with space. . . . We might almost say that space has been our time; at least it was until we filled up the space.[10]

Unlike most students of American culture, Nuhn singles out, not merely the quality of the physical environment, but its actual extent, as the shaping element of both the native culture and the native character.

> The point here is the nature of the new American unconsciousness, which must be studied shallow in historical time, or not at all. Its density is in the space dimension, a product of movement rather than status, and of interrelation rather than some single-line heredity. . . . If you are looking for it in

some "deeper" background back of the American background, you will only find something else—the old colonial character, or some other national character, or no character at all.[11]

The tension thus observed to exist between space-consciousness and time-consciousness is resolved into a series of polarities in American culture. Space itself is divided into East and West. A Western orientation represents fidelity to the principle of space; an Eastern one, the desire to return to the stream of time. The expansive quality of the national character is readily connected with the idea of equalitarianism; infatuation with time signifies a care for heredity, hence for the aristocratic idea. West means work and function; East means ornament and form. The matrix of the East-West dichotomy is the relation of Europe and America, Europe representing true East and America true West. In the light of this hypothesis about the composition of American culture, Nuhn perceives two main strands in American writing: the one oriented in space, hence faithful to the elemental character of culture; the other oriented in time, beguiled by the glamour of Europe, which in the end can only vitiate native literary talent.

My point has to do with moving and stopping in space, and it is not hard to see two streams verging off always from a central current. In one stream move the figures that respond to the new space. . . . On the far edge of this stream are the folks that always moved on. . . . The Western sky always looked rosy. . . . Then there is the other stream, and the figures in it are those that mostly felt they had come down, coming across, and saw the new space as empty and flat, the "terrible denudation" that James talked about. They kept their faces turned back over their shoulders, and sometimes turned around and went back.[12]

Nuhn's emphasis on environment and his discarding of tradition as alien to the native American character are

133

related to the primitivist concept of culture and nature as conflicting forces. The parallel is suggested by Nuhn's observation on a stock theme of American writing. "George F. Babbitt and Woodrow Wilson and Daisy Miller are alike in being easily confused by time and evil.... This situation of the time-innocent American confronted with the evils of history, is one of the standard situations in our cultural drama."[13]

The bifurcation of human activity into culture and nature, the identifying of Europe with culture and America with nature, both derive from an older, somewhat outmoded conception of culture as an artifice threatening man's innocence. The idea corresponds to a folk image, imbedded in the American consciousness, of Europe as the incarnation of evil. This image appears in American letters under various guises and on several levels of sophistication. It operates, for example, in the "international scene" created by Henry James.

> The motivating ideas of most of the novels of Henry James might be summarized very briefly, and perhaps a trifle crudely, as follows: that there is a moral sense, a sense of decency inherent in human character at its best; that this sense of decency, being only a sense, exists precariously, and may become confused and even hysterical in a crisis; that it may be enriched and cultivated through association with certain environments; that such association may, also, be carried so far as to extinguish the moral sense.... If we carry these generalizations a little further into the special terms of his novels, we find, however: that the moral sense as James conceives it is essentially American or at least appears to James most clearly in the American character; that it can be cultivated by association with European civilization and manners; that it may be weakened or in some other manner betrayed by an excess of such association.[14]

For a long time James had been rated in literary histories as the classic instance of the back-trailer, the expatriate writer who, having severed his home ties, dissipated his talent in works wholly alien to the native genius. One accomplishment of the massive James revival in the past thirty years is his reinstatement in the native canon. The motive of American innocence versus European sophistication indicates the authenticity of the native element in James's work. But the vindication of his work as a defense of the American character, made in several recent studies, probably errs in one direction just as the charge of disloyalty erred in the other. Europe and America, in James's imaginative world, are not employed as fixed counters: they are often charged with irony, as in *The Ambassadors;* they fluctuate in value from work to work, reflecting the ambiguity and complexity of his own relation to both Europe and America, a subject with which he was obsessed throughout his career.

The stresses involved in American-European intercourse provided an ideal subject for a writer whose principal theme was the interaction of culture and character. The international scene was a fabulous construction that could be variously manipulated to serve James's theme. Yet, allowing for the shifting values he attributed to America and Europe at different times, and also considering that he wrote novels, not sociological studies, we may discern the psychological substructure upon which the mythical construction is reared—the intellectual and emotional ambivalence toward Europe, peculiar, not only to his own personality and era, but also to the cultural tradition in which he participated and in which we participate. In that tradition Europe has stood for a positive as well as a negative value; James's idolatry of Europe is perhaps no less national than his allegory of American innocence and European depravity.

The appeal of Europe has been neither irresistible nor uniform in our literary culture. On the whole it is much more powerful there than in other aspects of our total culture, and it must be reckoned with as a preponderant force rather than an eccentricity. Contemporary criticism that either voices or implies resentment against Europe usually fails to recognize even the limited autonomy of literary culture; it expects literature to conform to a preconceived notion that hardly accords with the structure of modern culture. According to the sociologists, modern culture is composed of overlapping segments or strata, corresponding roughly to the multiple divisions of modern society—social, economic, professional, and regional. Stratification is incompatible neither with the theory of cultural integration (though stratified societies must necessarily be more loosely integrated than simpler societies), nor with the idea of a national configuration, provided the pattern is flexible enough to include a wide variety of differentiated traits. Unwilling to encompass such great diversity, the nationalist critic attempts to make American culture and American literature coalesce by reducing both to simpler designs. But he achieves their unification by excluding, according to predetermined standards of authenticity, much of our literary and cultural heritage.

The reductive propensities of nationalist criticism may be partly explained as evidence of the predilection already noted for homogeneous, primitive cultures. The critic's political views are also likely to have a bearing; for it is not easy to reconcile the stratification of culture with the democratic ethos, and least palatable to the democratic spirit is the class basis of culture. So far as any group in American society exhibits a pronounced deviation from the national norm or average, it is bound to be suspect. This sociological fact, as much as anything else, explains the hostility toward European culture in American criticism.

Sustained interest in Europe has been strongest within two distinguishable groups in American society—the one a social and economic class, the other a quasi-professional group that cuts across social and economic classes. The

136

first is the Northeastern patriciate that attained the height of its prestige during the second half of the nineteenth century. This class was unquestionably loyal; it was firmly rooted in the national life, and it had inherited its political and social ideals from the conservative party of the Revolution. The second is an intellectual and literary elite, mainly but not exclusively middle-class, mobile, far from homogeneous, therefore not easily defined. A self-elected group, among whose offices is the critical scrutiny of prevailing tastes and ideas, it is naturally unpopular, subject to severe hostility. Lacking social prestige, the literary elite has only an indirect influence on the whole culture.

The literary and intellectual elites are sometimes disposed of as eccentric outcroppings, with no organic relation to the society in which they appear. The patrician culture of the late nineteenth century is less easily dismissed, having been created by a class that had economic and political power, hence great social prestige. As the "Genteel Tradition," this culture became a target for the nationally oriented liberal criticism of the 'twenties. It is historically associated with the decline of New England culture, which had attained its peak by the mid-century. One infallible evidence of decline, according to Van Wyck Brooks, was the renewal of colonial feeling toward Europe. "New England had lost its political leadership. . . . [New Englanders] were uprooted and adrift in a world they did not understand. . . . They looked across the sea again, despairing of a nation that had passed beyond their power of comprehension. In their breasts rose once more the hankering for the ancient homeland, as if three generations of history had gone for nothing."[15] The critical realists easily discredited the effete culture of the New England twilight. Its most vulnerable point was its unproductiveness: it was imitative rather than creative, timid in the face of European achievement, sensitive to European opinion, smug in its cultural possessions, indifferent to the emergence of a native art.

137

Several features of this society and its culture are relevant to the discussion of the role of Europe in American letters. In politics genteel society was overtly hostile to the Jacksonian rabble, the plebeian democracy of the West; society was both fearful and contemptuous of the crude vigor of frontier America. These attitudes were hardly welcome to Westerners, who retaliated by writing off Eastern culture as aristocratic affectation. I speak, of course, of dominant attitudes; actually the West never lost its romantic hold on the East, just as the West, despite its pose, emulated the genteel culture of the East. In fact their relations are as ambivalent as those of European and American culture. In contemporary letters both the unregenerate expatriates and the most vociferous nationalists are likely to be Westerners. I suspect that excessive veneration for Europe and excessive hostility are both regional traits, more closely connected with the internal tensions of our society than with the realities of the American-European relation.

Today the whole movement of cultural nationalism in the United States is conditioned by reaction from Eastern upper-class culture, and particularly from the limited conception of culture. The nationalist view of culture, as originally connected with the life of society, is liable to important strictures; it has, however, discredited the older concept of culture as the possession of a privileged class, a meaning current since the Renaissance. So far as culture is identified with the insignia of rank, it is regarded as a product that the individual may acquire by expenditure of effort or money. "Culture," in the sense of individual taste or cultivation, is still current and still valid; but failure to correlate it with the broader meaning of the word promotes the spurious conception of art as a static phenomenon isolated from the culture of society as a whole.

The genteel attitude toward culture, which profoundly influenced the American literary climate in the nineteenth century and afterward, itself resulted from the

138

transformation in American society that took place about the time of the Civil War. Henry James accurately perceived the cultural implications of that change; he mentions "the great adventure of society reaching out into the apparent void for the amenities, the consummations, after having earnestly gathered in so many of the preparations and necessities." After two or more generations devoted to commerce, industry, and politics, a new middle class emerged, possessing for the first time means and leisure for the sort of culture that in European societies was the natural accompaniment of wealth and leisure. But whereas the European class cultures were generally founded upon an unbroken native tradition, this new class had no tradition of its own, or at least failed to realize its tradition. It members, having participated in the expansion of the country and the creation of a new industrial society, were repelled by the culture of the industrial metropolis and the frontier areas. According to their notion, the new culture was in fact non-culture—a cultural void. Believing that culture (refined cultivation) could be imported wholesale, they naturally reached toward Europe for the consummations and amenities mentioned by Henry James.

The cultural aspirations of the new American leisure class led (as the liberal economists, historians, and literary critics conclusively demonstrated) to a museum mentality that acknowledged only European culture and made the average American either indifferent to native art or contemptuous of it. Contempt for the native was intensified by the puritan strain in the genteel mentality which resisted the emergence of an art dealing with social realities.

> For by now, by 1870, the system of amenities dominated the province [New England]—and through the province, the literary standards of America. . . . A code of gentility, the twilight of religion, remained its last authority over America. The culture which . . . informed America was encapsuled from the real-

ities of American life and closed tight against everything passionate and disturbing in human experience. It was a cryptorchid culture and the literature
that expressed it was cryptorchid.[16]

The appropriation of "culture" by an exclusive group,
the tendency to identify it with European culture, and
the conviction that native conditions were somehow
antithetical to culture, all conspired to produce what
F. O. Matthiessen noted to be a permanent, tragic division in American life—"a culture whose greatest weak-
ness continued to be that our so-called educated class
knows so little of the country and the people of which it
is nominally a part."[17] The fissure is more evident, perhaps, to the student of literature than to other observers;
he knows it as a profound sense of alienation discernible
in American writing since the middle nineteenth century.
If not universal, the phenomenon has been far too widespread and persistent to dismiss as a minor aberration; it
makes itself felt even in writers who have powerfully
affirmed American life. The motives of alienation require
cautious treatment by the critic; generalization is here
particularly dangerous, and overt evidence misleading.
It is far too simple to construe alienation in terms of romantic escape on the one hand and of social protest on
the other.

The extreme act of the alienated artist was, of course,
expatriation. Again it is difficult to generalize; but for
some American artists expatriation was a radical experiment in culture founded upon the "genteel" conviction
that the native environment—materialistic in spirit,
equalitarian in politics, commercial in its engrossments—
was unfavorable or even hostile to the production of art.
The experiment was counterhistorical, an inversion of
the classic American experience. It has been described
by Van Wyck Brooks as the quest for the ancestral home.

For was not Redclyffe [in Hawthorne's *Doctor
Grimshawl's Secret*] the American heir, the first of
the transatlantic *revenants* that were to fill the nov-

els of Henry James? Irving and Longfellow, many another had felt the spell of the old world, but Redclyffe's nostalgia was something else than theirs: "The thought thrilled his bosom that this was his home—the home of the Western wanderer, who had gone away centuries ago, and encountered strange chances, and almost forgotten his origin, but still kept a clue to bring him back. . . . He began to feel the deep yearning which a sensitive American—his mind full of English thoughts, his imagination of English poetry, his heart of English character and sentiment—cannot fail to be influenced by,—the yearning of the blood within his veins for that from which it had been estranged. . . ."

In days to come, this feeling . . . was to play a part in American culture as marked as that of the "wanderers" of Pushkin's Russia. The most exotic writers hitherto had had the unquestioning instinct of homing pigeons, which brought them back from every foreign journey. The great tradition of the Revolution, the feeling of the national destiny, the prevalence of the classical studies that always made the mind its "own place," had rooted there in the western soil. . . . Then as the old causes grew dimmer and dimmer, as the European peasants arrived in thousands, as wealth advanced and tourists multiplied, as the human imagination felt cramped and thwarted in the vast industrial beehive . . . then this yearning for an older homeland rose in people's minds and men of sensibility flocked to Europe, not to study as in former days, and carry their spoils back, like traveling Romans, but as if they could ascend the river of time.[18]

Of all the American expatriates in the present century, only T. S. Eliot has fulfilled all specifications of the revenant. Deliberately and with full awareness of the cultural significance, symbolic and otherwise, of his act, he

141

renounced his native land for the mother country. The back-track motive, however, was no longer prominent in the wave of expatriation that followed the First World War. The Anglicanism of the patrician class, noted by Brooks, had been thinned out; European culture was now more likely to mean Continental culture. The new ideal was cosmopolitanism, and the American writer had been trained to abhor the provincial.

> His life until this time [1914] had been a long process of deracination. In the public schools he had been taught to avoid his native pronunciation, his idioms that smelled of the Nebraska soil, and to speak a sort of standardized Amerenglish. At the university he learned precisely nothing about the geography, government, economic life or local history of the region where he was born; instead he was introduced to that international republic of letters whose traditions are those of Athens, Florence, Paris, Berlin and Oxford. One effect of his studies was to place art and learning at an infinite distance from his daily life.[19]

Whereas some expatriates were bent upon acquiring fuller possession of the culture to which they had been exposed in the schools, some upon reclaiming a living cultural tradition, and some upon assimilating European culture within a native framework, the superficialities of the postwar cultural experiment are all too apparent. For the most part, expatriates failed to perceive the necessary social basis of culture. The pursuit of culture was often the counterpart of social irresponsibility; the writer not only revolted against the native values but wished to dispense altogether with the life of society. The patrician attitude toward European culture, dominant in the last decades of the nineteenth century, had gradually been converted into the bohemianism of a limited intellectual and artistic group no longer associated with a specific class. The defects of the bohemian mentality, as both the nativists and the critical realists were quick to point out,

were a disoriented eclecticism, an admiration for the
exotic as exotic, and an appetite for novelty and sensation. The literary temper of the years preceding the First
World War, implicit in the mood of many expatriates, is
described by Brooks:

> That Freud met no resistance was not his fault, and
> nothing met resistance in New York, where the doc-
> trines of the iconoclasts were sown broadcast. The
> brilliant journalist James Huneker spread before the
> younger minds the writings of Shaw, Nietzsche,
> D'Annunzio, Strindberg, Laforgue, Schnitzler,
> Wedekind, Anatole France, presenting them on one
> level. . . . All the native ideas seemed remote and
> dim beside this staggering onrush of new thoughts.
> These European writers floated in a vacuum—no
> critic related them to the native mind, and Huneker
> welcomed them all and passed them on with a sym-
> pathy and enthusiasm that knew no standards.[20]

In the immediate postwar years alienation had become
the rule; rejection of native culture and native values
assumed a violence and bitterness unprecedented in
American letters. Those who desired a vigorous, independent national culture viewed the prevailing temper
with alarm. In their analysis of the sources of alienation
Europe played a sinister role. The writer's estrangement,
which had originated in the unfavorable contrast between the poverty of American culture and the ampli-
tude of European, was being augmented by every fresh
contact overseas. Bohemian eclecticism and subservience
to European culture were both interpreted as reawaken-
ings of colonial inferiority.

Though the strictures of the liberal and nationalist
critics upon the colonial mentality were cogent and relevant, their program for a national literature underrated
the positive values of European culture and European
experience for the American. Expatriation can hardly be
defended as a normal strategy for the writer or artist; yet
it has sometimes proved more advantageous than injuri-

ous. Further, the actual experience of residence in Europe has been normal for American writers (the exceptions in the nineteenth century are surprising by their rarity—Thoreau, Whitman, Emily Dickinson, and a few more); by enriching the personal culture of innumerable American writers, it has enriched the national literature. The European experience acts upon the American writer in two ways. It reanimates the elements of European culture that are part of his own heritage, and it may of course intensify an existing state of alienation. But by placing in sharper relief the indigenous characteristics of his native culture, it can help him to realize their singularity more fully than he has done before. In other words, residence in Europe can make him more American: "His quality and background are tested in Europe as they are tested nowhere else; going to Europe thus becomes a cognitive act, an act of rediscovery and repossessing one's heritage."[21]

The impact of European culture upon American letters is a topic immense in scope and not amenable to easy generalizations. The premature excommunication of Henry James serves as a warning against a priori judgments. Clearly, European culture exists as both a negative and a positive element in American writing; to determine its effect, we must examine the individual writer or, better still, the individual work. A theory that prescribes the propriety or impropriety of European elements in American writing prescribes in effect the constitution of literary works, thereby ignoring the actualities of performance. In this sense it is antiliterary. So also are the various theories in which this prescription may figure: the requirement that American writing must conform to a cultural image derived primarily from social history; the notion that literary culture should coincide with popular culture; the regionalist position that relates national character to pioneer experience, denying authenticity to aberrations from the type.

Speculation about the national culture has increased

our understanding of the writer's vital and generic relation to his milieu. When, however, a theory of national culture reduces literary excellence to a single type or category and when it fails to allow for deviation (even wide deviation) from the national norm, it hinders rather than promotes the study of literature. The excellence of Henry James detracts in no way from the excellence of Mark Twain; the writings of both are inalienable possessions. It is the nature of literature both to fall short of and to transcend national culture; the perfectly national work does not exist. Somewhere in *The Times of Melville and Whitman,* Van Wyck Brooks paradoxically observes that Mark Twain's contribution to American culture was ignorance. He means that in a period when our literary culture was slavishly imitative, bound by European standards, it was salutary to have a writer who was either unaware of those standards or defiant. In other words, provinciality in a writer can be a positive virtue. Conversely, it can be argued that when the native standards become coercive, the American writer should become more, not less, cosmopolitan: "In one sense to be an 'American' is also to be concerned with European cultures; in that sense Ezra Pound and T. S. Eliot are never more 'American' than when they are most 'European.' "[22]

The ambiguity of the term "provincial" in literary discourse illustrates a certain confusion about the relation between European and American culture. Normally "provincial" denotes a limited or restricted attitude, removed from the main stream of activity and ideas. It signifies an eccentric state of mind. This meaning occurs in the following definition. "Provincialism is, of course, not a matter of literacy or illiteracy; it is a matter of attitude to the world at large. In its last analysis it is nothing more nor less than an *unawareness* of the process and kind of life in other orders."[23] In another context, however, the meaning is reversed and "provincial" signifies, not a limited awareness, but excessive awareness of what is going on in other parts of the world.

Roderick Hudson . . . went to Italy and soon lost what native promise he had, for he lost his own character. Garland needed to go only as far as Boston. The older, more finished society upset the new uncertain character, and the artistic impulse evaporated when the feeling for traditional conformity came in. . . . The irony was, as it always is, that the author in his late propriety became the provincial which he only feared he was earlier, for propriety— that is, somebody else's standards of good taste— is always the standard of the provincial. My point, of course, is not that character in one place is truer or better than character in another, but that one can be true only to his own character.

The unorthodox meaning here assigned to "provincial" is apparently related to an equally unorthodox conception of "standards." Criticism, inasmuch as it attempts to discern excellence, must be based upon standards. "Somebody else's standards" is a tautology; to speak of a standard based on fidelity to one's own character is to deny the possibility of criticism. The concept of national culture as a closed system, autonomous within geographic, political, or historical boundaries, may be relevant to the topic of literary causation; but it is too readily converted into a belief that fidelity to the national character is an adequate literary standard. Though the idea of universality is seriously challenged by the doctrine of cultural relativity, the critic is rationally bound to derive his standards from the widest possible cultural context. For the purpose of determining literary standards, culture ought not to mean less than the Western culture of the past two thousand years. Actually Western culture is more precariously situated than the national culture; the fears of the custodian of the national culture about foreign infiltration are probably groundless: cultures naturally tend to contract and become local, and it is the function of literature and intellect to counteract this tendency.

146

6

The Shape of Democratic Art

IN ONE SENSE no time is more remote from the present than the immediate past, no ideas more outworn than those of the preceding era. The privilege of supreme disillusion belongs to the present. We no longer perceive ourselves in what we were; our former certainties now appear to have been premature. Reputations are damaged in a single lifetime, none more than literary reputations. Theories also go into eclipse.

The political obsessions of critics in the 1930's seem now to have been compulsive, if not quite deranged. When questions of conscience become political—when to be nonpolitical is to be nonsentient—all human activities are likely to be viewed through political lenses. Literature is then described, explained, evaluated as an event in public life. But when, as now, public life engulfs those activities, the intellectual and moral role of politics is reduced. On the one hand, literature is perceived to embody moral orders that lie both above and below the level of public life; on the other, nonmoral properties in literature are reasserted and reëxamined. Currently the critical mode is inductive; it defends the integrity of works against prior judgment and grand generalizations. It teaches us to train our attention on the text and on internal evidence. A chapter of exegesis spent upon a single lyric discloses, not only the complexity of verbal art, but also the folly of reducing literature to one level of meaning, public or private.

The new perspective reveals the grosser aspects of the sociological method—its failure in discrimination, its heavy-handed determinism. Still, fastidiousness about "the act of criticism" cannot wholly exorcise the historical ghost from the literary body. The errors of the "political decade" in American criticism are grave: judgments were warped by extraliterary prejudices, and perception was surrendered to formula. Nevertheless, the transacted errors do not cancel the primary commitment of sociological criticism: the integration of literature in the life of society. Beyond this, it follows that the literary object cannot be seen steadily and whole apart from its social setting. The proper implementing of these propositions demands a kind of subtlety that has rarely been evinced by American sociological criticism: in particular it demands sensitivity to linguistic proprieties.

In American criticism during the 'thirties and for nearly a century before, the juxtaposition of the terms "literature" and "democracy" was almost automatic; it was made confidently and without self-consciousness.

> We maintain that the real meaning of the American social and cultural adventure has been its democratic meaning, and that one of the truest things to be said of American literature is that it has reflected over a period of three centuries, the gradual maturing, rationalization, and deepening of the democratic idea.[1]

Since 1936, when this statement was made, both the world and literary sensibility have changed—perhaps not enough to disturb its fundamental truth, but enough to call into question its forthrightness. We now doubt that either a culture or a literature can be summed up in a single term or that "reflect" properly describes their relation. Without question "democracy" is relevant to American culture, whose idiosyncrasy cannot be grasped apart from its political, economic, social forms and habits. And so far as literature participates in the life of society, American literature cannot have failed to be marked by democracy.

Granting this much, I suspect the indiscriminate labeling of a society, a culture, a literature with the same term. The phrase "democratic literature" names democracy as

148

an attribute of literary works, a quality felt and demonstrable in the form or the content, or both. The juxtaposition of "literature" and "democracy" may convey another meaning—not inconsonant with the previous one, yet distinct from it.

Emerson, Hawthorne, Thoreau, Whitman, and Melville all wrote literature for democracy in a double sense. They felt that it was incumbent upon their generation to give fulfillment to the potentialities freed by the Revolution, to provide a culture commensurate with American political opportunity. Their tones were sometimes optimistic . . . sometimes disillusioned, even despairing, but what emerges from the total pattern of their achievement—if we make the effort to repossess it—is literature for our democracy.[2]

The topics "democratic literature" and "literature for democracy," though obviously interdependent, belong to different areas of discourse. The first, referring to presumably concrete ascertainable data of literary works, lies within the province of criticism. The second pertains to matters anterior to criticism yet of prime interest to critics—the relations of literature and culture, of culture and society.

According to sociological criticism, literature is produced more or less directly by social conditions, of which it is a more or less accurate reflex. So far as the method is confined to exhibiting the social constituents of literary works, it is a valuable exegetical instrument. It will succeed in direct proportion to the explicitness of the social materials or motive in a given work; it is less capable in dealing with features that do not fall within easily recognized social categories or with works whose social significance is slight. Total submission to the method inevitably blinds the critic to wide regions of the imagination. The defect does not actually inhere in the method or its shortcomings. It proceeds from the fated disposition of method to convert itself into doctrine—in this instance, to fashion a literary philosophy from an insight into origins. Convinced that literature is a product of social circumstances, the critic identifies a condition of production with the purpose, and ultimately with the value, of the product. Despite perfunctory acknowledgment of literary (aesthetic) values, the work is judged finally on its efficacy as a mute record of past events or a spur to future activity.

The predominantly democratic character of American works is apprehended a posteriori both from the manifest forms of our society and from the prestige of democratic ideas in our political thought. In this context "democratic" is not neutral, but expresses a value judgment. We are persuaded to believe, not only that American literature is representative—hence democratic—but also that it should be so. The preceptive form in which the argument is phrased discloses irregularities in the deterministic process: apparently our literature does not perfectly represent our society. One main function of the critic is to distinguish the representative from the nonrepresentative and to bestow praise or blame accordingly. A closer examination of the writings of the sociological critics reveals that "democratic" does not stand for the whole environment but for specific preferences. Political orthodoxy is thus made a chief criterion of literary performance.

The risk incurred in criticism by any undivided preoccupation, whether political, psychological, or aesthetic, is narrowed sympathy—the failure to discern in literature qualities unrelated to the critic's special interests. This deficiency is conspicuous in V. L. Parrington, the most eminent sociological critic in American letters. Parrington's achievement was to reanimate the chronicle of our literature by situating it in the stream of events and ideas. But to a generation schooled in the theory of organic form, his competence is discredited by a disposition to locate the value and significance of works in their ideas (their paraphrasable content) and by his relegation of form, style, and structure to the limbo of belletristic ornament. Aside from aesthetic illiteracy, Parrington's criticism is reprehensible on its own grounds. His ideological purview, restricted to politics and economics, encompasses only a fraction of the moral and emotional range of literature. (In extenuation of Parrington, it should be recognized that in literary or cultural history abstraction is inevitable.)

Though the historian may cavil at Parrington's version of American politics—his economic determinism, his tendency to discover antinomies where none existed, his elevation of political dissent into an absolute virtue—his work still commands respect as a contribution to the history of ideas. It is praised also for creating "the first rounded progressive-democratic-social tradition for American writers to match the reactionary-aristocratic-religious tradition of Eliot, Ransom, Winters, et al."[3] No one can complain that Parrington fostered a narrowly sectarian tradition or that his political tastes were captious: despite his own rationalist, Populist, Jeffersonian bias, he embraced enthusiastically all native works that gave voice to liberal-democratic ideas. But whereas the aristocratic-religious tradition with which his criticism is contrasted is primarily literary, secondarily political and theological, Parrington's tradition is primarily political, secondarily literary. Artlessness led him to confound the imaginative and expository modes in literature. Imaginative writers operate by intuition, memory, perception, ambiguity, paradox. Parrington reduced imaginative works to a single level of meaning in order to use them as documentary exhibits in his own exposition of American social history and ideas. In one sense his tradition is the narrower of the two, since it is founded upon mutilation—it robs the contemporary writer of more valuable precedents than it supplies.

Although no tradition is viable for every age, and although each generation has to repossess and re-create

151

its inheritance, a literary tradition formed by ideological or political predilection is more than ordinarily subject to obsolescence. Parrington's political views, stemming from the broadest, most vigorous strain in American thought and temper, retain much of their vitality. But his literary authority has almost disappeared; his enthusiasms do not rouse an age that has become increasingly skeptical and introspective. Parrington's preferences and his readings of literary works were formed partly by a sensibility at once rebellious and optimistic; the liberal-democratic tradition that emerges from *Main Currents in American Thought* emphasizes the rebellious and optimistic elements in American writing more than is, perhaps, warranted by the facts. In the hands of the Marxist critics of the 'thirties, these elements were impaled upon a rigid formula.

> What stirs us in Emerson is his confidence in the common man, his courageous appeal for action, his faith in the future. He and Thoreau were rebels against the shams and oppressions of their day. . . . Whitman felt deeply his kinship with the workers and farmers. . . . Howells, James, and Mark Twain shrank from the cupidity of the gilded age. . . . Garland and Norris denounced oppression. . . . Sinclair and London called themselves socialists. This is the great tradition of American literature. Ours has been a critical literature, critical of greed, cowardice, and meanness. It has been a hopeful literature, touched again and again with a passion for brotherhood, justice, and intellectual honesty.[4]

The themes of social protest and of political idealism have indeed bulked large in American letters. But compressing a major tradition within their limits not only detracts from the plenitude of our literary past, but also cuts off the contemporary writer from his past by obscuring the continuity of the best writing of the present with the best writing of the past.

The notion of a democratic tradition in American letters is not peculiar to the critics of the left; it often occurs in criticism of a less pronounced political cast. Attempting to define the native literary tradition on lines broader than those used by the literary left, Henry Seidel Canby, for example, discerns certain permanent attributes: first, expansiveness, a trait shared by writers from Whitman to Wolfe; then—in the following order—equalitarianism, humanitarianism, reform, youthful energy. Thus far Canby's schedule fits the design urged upon us by most of the critics and literary historians who assign the significance of our literature to its democratic properties. But Canby notes a large breach in the quality of the tradition—"the curious duplex quality of the American imagination. Ever since the beginnings of our national literature this has been manifest. In the upper story we tend to be cheerful, generous, optimistic, humorous. But downstairs, writer after writer has been caught, sometimes fatally, by the macabre, the satiric, the sardonic, the horrible."[5]

This subterranean deposit in American writing has constantly embarrassed the liberal and the Marxist critics. Where it could not be stigmatized as alien, aristocratic, or pathological, it was glossed over or ignored, especially when visible in the work of writers who had been admitted to the democratic canon. To ignore it, however, was to falsify the record; to classify it as psychologically aberrant, as Parrington did in discussing Poe, was to obscure, not illumine, the nature and quality of our literary culture.

The introduction of sociological discipline in criticism had as its original motive the desire to avoid a wayward and arbitrary impressionism based on intuition or subjective tastes by establishing norms and standards derived from the literature of the past. One valid test of a theory so general as the social determination of literature is pragmatic. How well does it explain the particular phenomena of literature? Does it serve or impede that full, deliberate submission to the literary work that constitutes criticism? I suspect that the hypothesis that attempts to explain and evaluate American literature in terms of political norms (however admissible these may be) has not done justice to the actualities of a literature marked by obsession with violence and erosion almost from its beginnings.

The unanimity of a political belief among nineteenth-century American writers is a fiction promulgated by twentieth-century critics. Nevertheless, a strong case (on statistical grounds) can be made for the predisposition of American writers, both past and present, toward liberal democracy. But, as already noted, a writer's moral universe is not necessarily coextensive with his political convictions. Even in nineteenth-century literature the vocal native optimism was not unalloyed with skepticism and despair. The literature of social protest, which appeared late in the century and proliferated in the first decades of the twentieth century, did not (as Parrington and other critics liked to believe) issue solely from a militant, liberal impulse. It was sometimes the product of suffering and disillusion, compounded of both aspiration and disgust.

The designation of the fundamental quality of American literature by a political term is linked with a literary philosophy that correlates positively social history and literature; this approach tends to minimize or neglect evidence that undermines the initial premise. The result is an incapacity to manage literary properties that are unrelated to the central argument or counter to it. Literature is stripped of symbolic power and all dimensions except that of the flat, unambiguous statement. And if, in addition, the sociological method is used to implement a positive political program, the dereliction of criticism is completed.

Since the natural orbit of literature is morals, politics gets into literature as legitimately as another subject. Objection to a political interpretation of literature is not

154

therefore to be taken as a derogation of the political subject. But the critic who specifies the virtue of literature to be moral or political efficiency does not fulfill his task unless the moral agency of literature can be related to intrinsic formal properties. It still remains to be demonstrated whether the democratic attributes of American literature exist apart from articulated political views. In other words, can form or style as well as subject matter be described as democratic?

The central figure for criticism that postulates the democratic core of American letters is Walt Whitman; justly so, since no American writer has voiced more eloquently or less ambiguously his faith in democracy—in the solidarity of mankind, the potential of life lived in a democratic society. The compound of social criticism and dynamic optimism in his writings was an ideal demonstration of the orthodoxy proposed by twentieth-century political critics. Actually Whitman's significance as a democratic writer transcends the importance assigned to his work by a merely didactic conception of literature. For his work adumbrates, perhaps for the first time, a democratic aesthetics. His poetics was the counterpart—the reflex, it might be said, of his revolutionary politics. It was derived through Emerson from transcendentalist monism, which, in asserting the identity of man and nature, implied the identity of art and nature. Whitman's discovery was the concept of form as function—later to be developed, as Lewis Mumford has observed, into the functional aesthetics of Greenough, Sullivan, and Wright. According to Whitman's theory, form is immediately created by emotion; so far as art approaches the condition of organic nature, poetic form will be spontaneous, unconscious, and—at best—automatic. Conversely, by depreciating conscious concern with form, Whitman's poetics denies the importance of craft, discipline, technique; in effect it denies the importance of form as the definitive attribute of art.

The political and social correlative of Whitman's

poetic theory is, remarkably enough, democratic society. In Whitman's mind, and in much subsequent American criticism, substance is distinguished from form as spontaneous utterance is distinguished from artifice and convention. Traditional forms and a preoccupation with technique, having been associated with aristocratic European societies, are held to be inapposite to a society that dispenses with forms. In this perspective Whitman's poetic theory constitutes a "democratic aesthetics." Short of proposing that a democratic art be formless, it distrusts the presence of formal properties. Similar ideas keep recurring in American criticism—in the notion, for example, that our literature is "powerful, shaggy, and unique"; in the widespread animus against the art of Henry James; in hostility toward the alleged Alexandrianism of much contemporary poetry and criticism.

The poetics of Whitman—a special example of romantic doctrine—has not exerted great influence upon contemporary verse, which for the most part deviates from the precedent set by Whitman. But the functionalist aesthetics, in somewhat altered form, often occurs in the criticism of American fiction. It is still too soon to speak of a "poetics" of fiction; the subject has hardly been broached. The difficulties attending the criticism of fiction inhere in the nature of the novel, a fairly recent genre, bewildering in variety of purpose and performance, and thus far intractable to codification. There is still a poverty of critical terms having specific reference to fiction. Though we deplore the semantic disorder generated by the classic-romantic dichotomy, neither of these terms is so ambiguous as "realism," which has thus far been the most important norm in the criticism of fiction.

In a general yet fundamental sense, all literature aspires toward realism, that is, toward literary or poetic truth. It may be assumed that the novel, during the most of its history, has developed rather steadily toward realism in the narrower sense of verisimilitude—the

156

method of representing reality. Thus delimited, the term still remains ambiguous. The nineteenth-century Continental novel, for example, was sometimes furnished with a doctrinal basis, a reasoned view of fiction in relation to general philosophic notions. But realism and naturalism, as practiced in the modern American novel, were apparently not informed by literary theory.

> Everything that is significant in the history of American realism stems from the fact, confirmable over fifty years of sub-literary experience, that while in Europe realism and naturalism grew out of the positivism of Continental thought and the conviction that one literary movement had subsided and another was needed, realism in America grew out of the bewilderment, and thrived on the simple grimness of a generation suddenly brought face to face with the pervasive materialism of industrial capitalism. Realism in Europe founds its philosophy in mechanism, its cosmogony in the Newtonian conception of the universe, its authority in Comte, Darwin, and Taine. Realism in America . . . poured sullenly out of agrarian bitterness, the class hatreds of the eighties and nineties, the bleakness of small-town life . . . and the bitterness in the great new proletarian cities. Realism came to America from everywhere and nowhere . . . and it had no center, no unifying principle, no philosophy, no joy in coming, no climate of experiment. There was something dim, groping, unrealized in American realism even when it found its master in Dreiser.[6]

The bulk of American realistic fiction embodies an attitude toward life, not toward the art of fiction. Whereas realism signified to Flaubert, Maupassant, Zola, and Henry James a conscious method of coping with reality, to most American writers it often meant an unmediated response to experience, particularly to social phenomena. There is a kinship between Whitman's poetics and the literary primitivism that characterizes the practice of

American novelists and that survives in the theoretical presuppositions of Howells, Frank Norris, Dreiser—novelists who were not ignorant of European theory. Removed from the realm of method and technique, realism in the novel means little more than fidelity to fact, the "passive documentation" of experience uninhibited by preconceptions of form or style. The form of fiction, in other words, is actually determined by the materials of experience. Yvor Winters, designating the notion as "the fallacy of imitative form," traces its origin to Emerson, who situated the source of knowledge in the intuitions and perceptions of the individual psyche. Emerson's doctrine is clearly relevant to the native ethos. It affirms self-reliance, the validity of individual judgment and perception, and inculcates a mistrust of tradition and technical skills.

It was Howells who formally enunciated the parallel between "realism" and the temper of democracy. Howells was concerned with the relation of literature and democracy in the double sense: the democratic properties of literature, and the status of literature in democratic culture. In the latter he voices the optimism of his time.

> I am in hopes that the communistic era in taste foreshadowed by Burke is aproaching, and that it will occur within the lives of men now overawed by the foolish old superstition that literature and art are anything but the expression of life, and are to be judged by any other test than that of fidelity to it.[7]

In denying the sectarian appeal of art and affirming the direct relation of art to experience, Howells reiterates Emerson's and Whitman's anticipatory account of democratic culture. His conception of literary realism is predicated upon the expressionistic thesis of Emerson and Whitman. Since literature is an "expression of life," it will be accessible to all who participate in the same experience. Experience is equated with the local and common. Realism—fidelity to experience—is thus construed as the literary mode both peculiar and proper to democracy. "Realism is the child of democracy because the realist is one who 'feels in every nerve the equality of things and the unity of men.' "

Though Howells's literary credo remained essentially unchanged, his later novels reveal a modification of realism in the direction of the "critical realism" championed by Parrington. According to the latter,

> While Henry James was moving towards aristocratic Mayfair, Howells was journeying towards the proletarian East Side. . . . Howells came late into an interest in sociology, held back by the strong literary and aesthetic cast of his mind. But in the eighties, when he had reached middle life, he was no longer able to ignore or evade the economic maladjustments of the Gilded Age.[8]

It is clearly implied here that Howells, in contrast with James, stood for democratic literature. But since James also considered his literary method to be realism— that is, fidelity to experience—"realism" obviously does not adequately indicate the distinguishing characteristic of democratic literature. The real clue to the distinction between democratic and aristocratic art is the stated antithesis of sociology and aesthetics.

The notion that form is determined by subject matter is not, after all, so far removed from the position of the sociological critic—namely, that form may be abstracted from content, and that only content is germane to literary judgment. The alternative to this position is not an aestheticism that bans the use of practical or moral criteria, but a literary method that respects both the integrity and the particularity of the work. The latter point of view takes into account, not only the dependency of literature upon experience, but also the signal difference between literature and experience. The "extrinsic" approach is founded upon the valid enough perception that the material of literature is reality or experience; but it fails to perceive that literary art is the medium for transmuting materials into something resembling reality and experience but no longer identical with them. In that difference, no matter how small it may seem, lies the indispensable autonomy of art.

Sociological criticism, a special example of the "extrinsic" method, goes on to identify reality and experience with social reality and social experience. When a critic asserts that American literature is or ought to be democratic, he implies that the primary value of literature lies in its usefulness, either as a passive record of social experience or as an agent of social change. But the reduction of literature to its social functions is nonempirical; this reduction misses the unique, nontransferable experience that only the literary work can provide. Contrary to the belief of sociological critics, respect for aesthetic autonomy is not equivalent to an antisocial attitude, nor need it involve indifference to the social functions of literature.

The liberal critics of the 'twenties and 'thirties, desiring a literature with the broadest possible social base, miscalculated the complexity of both literature and society by attempting to reduce both to political and economic formulas. Their motive was to some extent a desire to mend the alarming breach between literature and society in their own time. What they did not perceive was that literature exists only in an oblique relation to society, that the intermediate element is culture, and that the problem is not mainly political and economic but cultural.

The fullest exposition of a theory of art in the context of democratic ideas is John Dewey's *Art As Experience*. Dewey attacks the compartmental conception of art as a "spiritual" activity discontinuous with the other activities of a culture. For him the segregation of art in modern culture is not merely a sociological effect; it exemplifies the vast increase in specialization that has occurred in modern intellectual life and the consequent divorce of many cultural activities from the life of society. The reintegration of art in social life, if it is to be achieved, may not dispense with aesthetic integrity.

> Art is a quality that permeates an experience; it is not, save by a figure of speech, the experience itself. Esthetic experience is always more than esthetic. In it a body of matters and meanings, not in themselves esthetic, *become* esthetic as they enter into an ordered rhythmic movement towards consummation. . . . The material of esthetic experience in being human . . . is social. Esthetic experience is a manifestation, a record and celebration of the life of a civilization, a means of promoting its development, and is also the ultimate judgment upon the quality of a civilization. For while it is produced and enjoyed by individuals, these individuals are what they are in the content of their experience because of the culture in which they participate.[9]

Dewey does not, on the evidence of style or subject matter, discriminate between a social and an antisocial art; for aesthetic experience, a binding element in culture, is innately social.

> Experience strikes below the barriers that separate human beings from one another. Since art is the most universal form of language, since it is constituted, even apart from literature, by the common qualities of the public world, it is the most universal and freest form of communication. . . . The sense of communion generated by a work of art may take on a definitely religious quality. . . . Art is the extension of the power of rites and ceremonies to unite men, through a shared celebration, to all incidents and scenes of life. . . . That art weds man and nature is a familiar fact. Art also renders men aware of their union with one another in origin and destiny.[10]

The accents of Whitman and Emerson are heard in Dewey's generous estimate of the social potential of art. Unfortunately, contemporary culture does not seem to

161

have realized this potential. Instead of steady expansion, we have witnessed the growing attenuation of aesthetic experience in our society and a corresponding decline in the prestige of imagination as a cognitive mode. Our intellectual culture is overwhelmingly pragmatic and rational. The disparity between the aesthetic interests of the majority and of those seriously devoted to the arts, though not absolute, is profound.

To the protagonists of a "democratic literature" the very existence of works produced for a minority and exclusively admired by a minority seems to menace the foundations of democratic culture. This conviction is evidently founded on an exaggerated and unhistorical notion of the uniformity of culture as well as on a mechanistic view of cultural determination. The critics who propose to employ the social potential of literature deliberately, thus effecting a culture commensurate with the social aims of democracy, underestimate the initiative and momentum possessed by the various cultural activities within a society.

The main proposition that culture is produced by society cannot well be contested. As Karl Mannheim said,

> Social forces always find expression in culture, even when they work unseen, and the problem is falsely stated if society and culture are torn apart from one another and are regarded as fully independent spheres which, as such, react upon one another. The social process is contained in the very structure of cultural life itself, so that it is never for one moment free from its influence.[11]

But it is incorrect to infer from the integral relation of society and culture that their structures are identical or that cultural change is automatically determined by social. In the same paragraph Mannheim continues: "In every society of a certain degree of complexity, cultural life not only develops its own institutions but even seems to exist in a world apart which does, indeed, in many respects have a continuity all its own." In a discussion of the culture of modern democracies, this second observation of Mannheim's—the hypothesis concerning the actual though limited autonomy of culture—would seem more relevant than the first one.

The problematical nature of the term "culture" in current discourse results, according to T. S. Eliot (*Notes towards a Definition of Culture*), from its indiscriminate reference to three distinct though interdependent phenomena: the culture of the individual, the culture of the group, and the culture of society. In the third and largest sense, culture denotes a society's total way of life—the subject matter of the cultural anthropologist. Mannheim is evidently dealing with a more limited concept—the conscious intellectual and aesthetic culture created, fostered, and transmitted by specialized elites in modern liberal-democratic societies. The idea of cultural elites was naturally repugnant to the nineteenth-century liberal mind, which was unalterably opposed to social elites or aristocracies. Just as naturally, it was expected that the social and political order newly created in the United States would produce a high universal culture. Emerson and Whitman, for example, easily transposed the democratic idea from society to culture, which was then regarded as a desideratum acquired by voluntary individual effort. The artificial barriers of social inequality having been removed, the members of a democratic society would aspire to the highest culture of which they were capable and would eventually possess it.

The cultural outlook of Emerson and Whitman was firmly rooted in the liberal-romantic temper. It was founded upon a thoroughly generous and optimistic view of human nature—man's perfectibility. But even within their lifetimes, hope had begun to dim. The shape of the industrial society that was beginning to emerge in the United States gave grounds for doubt. Does an increase in social equality and individual freedom proportionately raise the general level of culture? Does it lead to a universal culture of high order? Today, of course, we know what Emerson and Whitman could not know: the character of a mass culture established upon the facts of universal literacy and relatively free access to cultural products.

The transformation of American society since the time of Emerson and Whitman has fulfilled their prophecies in one respect. Apologists for mass culture cite the enormous increase in the consumption of "cultural goods" in the present century. But statistical evidence of the widespread diffusion of culture is not in itself proof of vitality; the creative capacities of a culture may even be frustrated by large-scale mechanical diffusion. The apparent contradiction is resolved if a distinction is made between culture that may be acquired by voluntary effort and the culture in which the individual participates by virtue of his membership in society. Culture in the latter sense is an integrated whole that contains the aggregate of its component parts yet transcends the aggregate. Forming as it does the substratum of personality, the collective culture predetermines the individual's capacity for cultural realization. Although the individual can exercise choice, his freedom is no guarantee that he will make the best possible choice. An illuminating example is the translation of the peasant from his native village, with its fixed tradition of style and design, to the metropolis, where the possibilities of choice are far greater. Almost inevitably he will prefer the aesthetically inferior articles of industrial civilization to those with which he has been familiar. Without entirely discounting individual variations in taste and judgment, we are led to infer that these powers are formed primarily by a cultural tradition.

Although the culture of the United States has certainly not developed along lines predicted nearly a century ago, it would be rash to describe—much less to judge—contemporary American culture in the largest sense. Our literary culture alone is baffling in its complexity, though the criteria required to assess literary culture are not many. They may be reduced to two: the size of the audience for literature, and the quality of the literature produced.

Questions concerning literary standards and the relation of artist to audience in past cultures are not easily solved. But the contemporary situation is unprecedented in both the structure of society and the nature of modern art. There is little doubt that the complex societies of the past exhibited greater integration than society today. Yet many who criticize the present tend to read into former literary cultures more homogeneity than they actually possessed. At very few moments in history has the writer been able to produce works that fully engaged his capabilities as craftsman and creative artist, with no sacrifice of integrity or compromise with standards, and at the same time to satisfy the fundamental and common interests of his society. Literature has usually been produced for a limited audience, the writer being under no illusion that he was addressing the entire population. And until a century ago the writer was more or less aware of the social identity of his public. In our time the levels of literary culture no longer correspond to well-defined social strata, and literature of the highest order no longer engages the full interest of any considerable segment of society.

It is far too simple to blame the contemporary cultural situation on the atomization of society, for the cause lies also in the nature of the best modern literature—its singular failure to make any claim on the majority of those devoted to ideas and morality. In a study entitled "Avant-Garde and Kitsch," Clement Greenberg has demonstrated that the current situation represents a new and radically different alignment of cultural elements rather than a deterioration of former patterns. The art of the avant-garde, for example, is a new element made possible by "a superior consciousness of history—more precisely, the appearance of a new kind of criticism of

165

society, an historical criticism." Armed with this awareness, the artist no longer unconsciously plays the part of spokesman for the community; he conceives his role, first as one of active opposition to society, and finally as one quite apart from society.

> In turning his attention away from the subject matter of common experience, the poet or artist turns it upon the medium of his own craft.... The avant-garde's specialization of itself, the fact that its best artists are artists' artists ... has estranged a great many of those who were capable formerly of enjoying and appreciating ambitious art and literature, but who are now unwilling or unable to acquire an initiation into their craft secrets. The masses have always remained more or less indifferent to culture in the process of development. But today such culture is being abandoned by those to whom it actually belongs—our ruling class.[12]

The other new element in modern culture relates to popular art, or what Greenberg calls "Kitsch." The characteristic popular art of our era is a joint product of universal literacy and industrial technology. Whereas authentic folk art is a relatively spontaneous product of the aesthetic and cultural interests of a people, distinguished from serious or sophisticated art in manner but not in kind, contemporary popular art is a commodity made possible by the rationalization of industry. Though usually regarded as merely a debased form of art, Kitsch is said by Greenberg to lack the purposive aesthetic element that characterizes art.

An account of the realities of American literary culture reveals, not the universal culture envisaged by the romantic writer of the past or the social architect of the present, but a sharp stratification of tastes and interests. The literate masses, deprived of the aesthetic discipline acquired by oral and visual means in primitive and folk societies, are either indifferent to the distinction between the aesthetic and nonaesthetic or incapable of making the distinction. The enormous quantity of printed matter designed specifically for this audience does not ordinarily fall into the category of literature as normally conceived by the literary student.

Farthest removed from the masses in culture, though not necessarily in society, are what Mannheim calls the elites—highly specialized minorities actively or professionally concerned with literature and literary standards. According to Richard Chase, serious literary preoccupation is now confined to small islands within the educated class—the academy, the nonacademic liberal left, and the nonacademic advance guard. But even within these islands there is little homogeneity or stability. The academy is conservative, assimilating rather slowly the attitudes of the advanced elements in our culture. The liberal left either has made interest in literature ancillary to political ends or, recoiling from politics, has merged with the advance guard. The advance guard in turn is split, though not decisively, between experiment and tradition, socialism and a hierarchical society, naturalism and Christian orthodoxy.

Lying between the elites and the masses is that large, amorphous aggregate of "common readers"—the remainder of the educated class. The singularity of its culture—which is often inaccurately identified with the whole culture—is an almost complete devaluation of art and imagination as forms of knowledge. In such a culture literature no longer has the prestige it formerly enjoyed; the passivity of our educated class toward literature signifies a defection from what R. P. Blackmur has called the "cultural adventure" of our time.

The split between theory and practice, frequently noted as a primary characteristic of the native ethos, is particularly evident in discussions of our literary culture. The American social structure is fluid, so that the individual can shift his status with far greater ease than in the fixed-status societies of the past or, for that matter, in contemporary societies where the hierarchical struc-

167

ture exists in vestigial form. There is, however, a general reluctance to admit the discrepancy between the theory of social equality and the reality of social stratification in the United States. The dynamics of our social structure obscures the situation as it concerns culture. Since the potentialities of the individual are conditioned by the group, the stratification of modern complex societies is a powerful limiting factor in the formation of a universal national culture.

The so-called crisis in American culture, therefore, results neither from failure to achieve complete homogeneity (there is at any rate no precedent for such homogeneity in Western history) nor from the existing division of cultural labor, but rather from the peculiar relation of culture and society in our time. Here the insight of Mannheim is valuable.

> It seems to be a sociological principle that the social value of intellectual culture is a function of the social status of those who produce it. It not only took a long time for intellectual culture as such to attain general recognition, but in the course of this development the rank in society of those who produced it was time and again decisive for the value which was placed upon it. . . . We know from Greek history that the plastic arts were looked down upon for a long time because those engaging in these arts were originally slaves.[13]

The problem in liberal democratic society is not solved by the eradication of elites and the reduction of culture to one uniform level; this would abrogate the achievements of the intellect and annul the distinctive, traditional properties of imaginative literature. The main difficulty, rather, appears to be the preservation of cultural elites. On the one hand, modern life and thought have brought about the fragmentation of an intellectual class into groups whose members have in common only an extremely specialized interest. On the other hand—such is the fluidity of democratic society—the elites cannot perpetuate themselves long enough to make a permanent impression on the remainder of society. According to William Phillips, the record of American letters is one of recurring frustration of the attempt to form an independent intellectual tradition. The peculiar pressure operating upon the American writer is a sense of guilt induced by the Populist myth that causes him to forfeit his identity and submerge himself in the mass.[14]

The proposition that culture flourishes best in a hierarchical society, however persuasive, has little practical relevance either to modern culture or to modern society. The graded society admired by T. S. Eliot and his colleagues exists, not as an alternative to liberal society, but only as a speculative exercise. Yet the severity of the traditionalist sociology serves as a check on the wishfulness that, by analogical reasoning, predicates a vital and robust culture on an equalitarian society. In the past two decades we have heard the charge of decadence leveled against liberal-democratic culture by societies in which the attempt has been made to create homogeneous and uniform cultures through forced growth. The real alternative to democratic culture involves a social structure in which every phase of life is controlled and regulated by institutional organization. In such societies the social relevance of literature is assured; indeed, social utility becomes the sole criterion of culture. Needless to say, the prospect of state control and supervision of culture is abhorrent to nearly all American critics, including those who most deplore the existing condition of culture.

In order to undermine the argument for a reorientation of literature on social lines I have perhaps insisted too much upon the fallacy of uniformity. For the most part, liberal critics have desired a unified rather than a uniform culture. Now it is generally agreed that a vigorous literary culture depends upon the integration and coherence of the general culture of society, without which there can be no healthy culture for either the individual or the group. But even so, the liberal critics have ima-

169

gined certain activities to be replicas of the basic culture of society and have tended to underestimate the need for diversity of culture. Eliot has demonstrated convincingly that, within certain limits, diversity and even friction between various elements are a necessary condition of a live culture. Proponents of social realism and literary nationalism both overemphasize the generic aspects of culture and slight the nuances of individuality in literature. They fail to conceive of an integrated culture encompassing, not only great diversity, but even wide deviations from a norm. It seems to be the nature of society—even a relatively nonrepressive society—to produce a leveling effect upon ideas, manners, and taste. In certain periods may it not be a function of literature to prevent a society from becoming overwhelmingly assertive?

Even though we perceive the frailties of contemporary literary culture, we should be grateful for one necessary condition that our political system provides—the means for diversity. The democratic state, though it may not actually encourage variety, is not formally committed to eradicating it. And so long as this condition is maintained, individuals and groups will continue to hand on the legacy of the past—the standards of excellence, the techniques and disciplines without which culture as we have known it cannot survive.

Modern speculation on culture tends to undervalue the individual's contribution and to emphasize the social coördinates of culture. Salutary as this tendency has been, it should not obscure the all-important fact, which we have sometimes lost sight of, that culture is ultimately created by individual acts.

> The artist, we have admitted, is a unit of a necessary social organization and cannot arrive even at the threshold of his potentialities without the condition which a culture provides. But having reached that threshold, he must be left to proceed alone, as an individual.[15]

Whether or not it is too late for the individual, proceeding alone, to consummate the acts of culture is more than we can know; but we do know that individual acts are no longer possible except in democracies.

The reconstitution of culture is probably beyond the means of voluntary planning and certainly beyond political means. Is there then no alternative to fatalism? Must the individual resign himself to passivity? Turning this question to the specific subject of the status of literature in an era of disintegration—what is the proper role of the individual writer and critic? An answer is suggested by the peculiar ambivalence of both literature and the individual writer in relation to culture. The individual is in bondage to his culture; hence art, up to a point, is determined by culture. But the creative artist, more than most men, still retains a certain initiative. How can he employ it?

He may, if he still believes that culture can be restored by individual acts, stake everything upon the social acceptance of his work and its social utility, thereby abandoning some qualities of literary art that, having acquired great value in our culture, are constitutive in the culture. The risk in this undertaking is that the effect of social intent will be social; it may not necessarily serve culture. The alternative for the modern artist is the quixotic resolve to surmount his destiny by an act of faith—fidelity to his art, its standards, tradition, and potentialities, without respect to its viability in society—and thus to fulfill what André Malraux believes always to have been the permanent, specifically human function of the artist.

Both alternatives have a profound meaning for the future, not only of American culture, but of what we call Western culture. The persistence of either alternative points toward the extinction of art, the first by default, the second by an excess of devotion. Should this occur, culture as we know it will also disappear. And we cannot, in the light of history, rule out the possibility that this disappearance is ineluctable. But whether or not the event be imminent, one thing is clear: literature will be the last of the arts to fail. For even in an era of cultural disintegration the primary function of literature as art can never be totally deprived of social meaning so long as the integrity of an art involves the integrity of its medium. Since language is the intermediary by which literature and society are directly and reciprocally related, devotion to the literary medium fully implicates the writer in social awareness.

Notes

CHAPTER 1.

[1] Alfred Kazin, *On Native Grounds* (New York, Reynal and Hitchcock, Inc., 1942), p. ix. Quotations used by permission of Harcourt, Brace and Co., Inc.

[2] Van Wyck Brooks, "America's Coming of Age," in *Three Essays on American* (New York, E. P. Dutton and Co., Inc., 1934), p. 41. Quotations used by permission of the publisher.

[3] *Ibid.*, p. 105.

[4] *Ibid.*, p. 60.

[5] Vernon L. Parrington, *Main Currents in American Thought* (New York, Harcourt, Brace and Co., Inc., 1930), III, 53. Quotations used by permission of the publisher.

[6] Ludwig Lewisohn, *Expression in America* (New York, Harper and Bros., 1932), p. 117. Quotations used by permission of the publisher.

[7] Van Wyck Brooks, *op. cit.*, p. 85.

[8] Vernon L. Parrington, *op. cit.*, p. 86.

[9] *Ibid.*, p. 87.

[10] Ludwig Lewisohn, *op. cit.*, p. 505.

[11] T. K. Whipple, *Spokesmen* (New York, Appleton-Century-Crofts, Inc., 1928), p. 90. Quotations used by permission of the publisher.

[12] *Ibid.*, p. 112.

[13] *Ibid.*, p. 122.

[14] *Ibid.*, p. 158–159.

[15] *Ibid.*, p. 182.

[16] *Ibid.*, p. 224.

[17] *Ibid.*, p. 250.

[18] *Ibid.*, p. 43.

[19] William Phillips, "The Intellectuals' Tradition," *Partisan Review*, Vol. VIII, No. 6 (Nov.-Dec., 1941), p. 491. Quotations used by permission of the *Partisan Review.*

[20] Harold Stearns, *Civilization in the United States: An Inquiry by Thirty Americans* (New York, Harcourt, Brace and Co., Inc., 1922), p. vii. Quotations used by permission of the publisher.

[21] H. L. Mencken, "Puritanism as a Literary Force," in *A Book of Prefaces* (New York, Alfred A. Knopf, Inc., 1922), pp. 198–199.

[22] Ludwig Lewisohn, *op. cit.*, p. xxiv.

[23] *Ibid.*, pp. 154–159.

[24] *Ibid.*, p. xxxi.

[25] Alfred Kazin, *op. cit.*, p. 156.

[26] "American Fiction: The Major Trend," *Proletarian Literature in the United States* (New York, International Publishers, 1935).

[27] Herbert Croly, "Henry James and His Countrymen," *in* F. W.

Dupee, *The Question of Henry James* (New York, Henry Holt and Co., Inc., 1945). Quotations used by permission of the publisher.

[28] Waldo Frank, *Our America* (New York, Boni and Liveright, 1919), p. 74. Quotations used by permission of Liveright Publishing Corp., copyright renewed Waldo Frank, 1947.

[29] F. W. Dupee, *op. cit.*, p. xii.

[30] Henry James, "The Madonna of the Future," *in* F. O. Matthiessen, ed., *Stories of Writers and Artists* (New York, New Directions, 1944), p. 21. Quotations used by permission of the publisher.

[31] R. P. Blackmur, *in* R. E. Spiller, W. Thorp, T. H. Johnson, H. S. Canby, eds., *Literary History of the United States* (New York, The Macmillan Co., 1948), p. 1,039. Quotations used by permission of the publisher.

[32] Henry James, *Hawthorne* (New York, Harper and Brothers, 1879), p. 3. Quotations used by permission of the publisher.

[33] *Ibid.*, p. 29.

[34] *Ibid.*, pp. 30–31.

[35] Matthew Josephson, *Portrait of the Artist as an American* (New York, Harcourt, Brace and Co., Inc., 1930), p. xvii. Quotations used by permission of the publisher.

[36] D. H. Lawrence, *Studies in Classic American Literature* (New York, The Viking Press, Inc., 1924), p. 73. Quotations used by permission of the publisher.

[37] Newton Arvin, "Individualism and the American Writer," *Nation*, Vol. CXXXIII, No. 391 (Oct. 14, 1931), p. 391. Quotations used by permission of the *Nation*.

[38] James T. Farrell, *A Note on Literary Criticism* (1936).

[39] V. F. Calverton, *The Liberation of American Literature* (New York, Charles Scribner's Sons, 1932), p. 474. Quotations used by permission of the publisher.

[40] William Barrett, "Writers and Madness," *Partisan Review*, Vol. XIV, No. 1 (Jan.-Feb., 1947), p. 21.

[41] William Phillips, "Dostoevsky's Underground Man," *ibid.*, Vol. XIII, No. 5 (Nov.-Dec., 1946), pp. 551–552.

[42] Philip Rahv, "Concerning Tolstoi," *ibid.*

[43] F. O. Matthiessen, *The Achievement of T. S. Eliot: An Essay on the Nature of Poetry* (New York, Oxford University Press, Inc., 1935), p. 42. Quotations used by permission of the publisher.

[44] Morton D. Zabel, *Literary Opinion in America* (New York, Harper and Brothers, 1937), p. xxvi. Quotations used by permission of the publisher.

CHAPTER 2.

[1] G. V. Plekhanov, *Art and Society* (New York, Critics' Group Series No. 3, 1936).

[2] Morris R. Cohen, *Reason and Nature: An Essay on the Meaning of Scientific Method* (New York, Harcourt, Brace and Co., Inc., 1931), p. 386. Quotations used by permission of Felix S. Cohen.

[3] William Aylott Orton, *America in Search of Culture* (Boston, Little, Brown and Co., 1933. Quotations used by permission of the author.

CHAPTER 3.

[1] Malcolm Cowley, *Exile's Return* (New York, The Viking Press, Inc., 1951), p. 107. Quotations used by permission of the publisher.

[2] Irving Babbitt, *Rousseau and Romanticism* (Boston, Houghton Mifflin Co., 1919), p. 48. Quotations used by permission of the publisher.

[3] Rebecca West, *Black Lamb and Grey Falcon* (New York, The Viking Press, Inc., 1941). p. 842. Quotations used by permission of the publisher.

[4] Howard Mumford Jones, *Ideas in America* (Cambridge, Mass., Harvard University Press, 1945. Quotations used by permission of the publisher.

[5] Van Wyck Brooks, "America's Coming of Age," in *Three Essays on America* (New York, Dutton, 1934), p. 83.

[6] Van Wyck Brooks, "Letters and Leadership," in *Three Essays on America*, pp. 156, 166.

[7] L. Cazamian, *in* E. Legouis and L. Cazamian, *A History of English Literature* (New York, The Macmillan Co., 1935), pp. xvi–xvii. Quotations used by permission of the publisher.

[8] A. Kardiner and R. Linton, *The Psychological Frontiers of Society* (New York, Columbia University Press, 1945), pp. vii, xvi. Quotations used by permission of the publisher.

[9] Howard Mumford Jones, *op. cit.*, p. 30.

[10] Henry Seidel Canby, foreword to Claude M. Simpson and Allan Nevins, *The American Reader* (Boston, D. C. Heath and Co., 1941), pp. v–vii. Quotations used by permission of the publisher.

[11] Constance Rourke, *The Roots of American Culture* (New York, Harcourt, Brace and Co., Inc., 1942), p. 294. Quotations used by permission of the publisher.

[12] *Ibid.*, p. 50.

[13] *Ibid.*, p. 284.

[14] *Ibid.*, pp. 288, 294.

[15] B. A. Botkin, *Folk-Say I* (Norman, University of Oklahoma Press, 1929), pp. 14, 15. Quotations used by permission of the publisher.

[16] *Ibid.*, p. 16.

[17] T. K. Whipple, *Study Out the Land* (Berkeley and Los Angeles, University of California Press, 1943), pp. 15–16.

[18] *Ibid.*, p. 62.

[19] *Ibid.*, p. 59.

[20] Constance Rourke, *op. cit.*, pp. 285–286.

[21] Van Wyck Brooks, *The Flowering of New England* (New York, E. P. Dutton and Co., Inc., 1936; London, J. M. Dent and Sons, Ltd., 1936), pp. 420–421. Quotations used by permission of the publishers.

[22] Wallace Stegner, "Regionalism in Art," *Delphian Quarterly* (Jan., 1939). Quotations used by permission of the author.

[23] Van Wyck Brooks, *The Flowering of New England*, p. 51.

CHAPTER 4.

[1] Van Wyck Brooks, *New England: Indian Summer* (New York, E. P. Dutton and Co., Inc., 1940; London, J. M. Dent and Sons, Ltd., 1940), p. 524. Quotations used by permission of the publishers.

[2] Merle Curti, *The Roots of American Loyalty* (New York, Columbia University Press, 1946), p. 23. Quotations used by permission of the publisher.

[3] Wallace Stegner, "Regionalism in Art," *Delphian Quarterly* (Jan., 1939),

[4] Donald Davidson, *The Attack on Leviathan* (Chapel Hill, The University of North Carolina Press, 1938), p. 52. Quotations used by permission of the publisher.

[5] Lewis Mumford, *Faith for Living* (New York, Harcourt, Brace and Co., Inc., 1940), pp. 117–118. Quotations used by permission of the publisher.

[6] John Crowe Ransom, "The Esthetic of Regionalism," *in* M. D. Zabel, *Literary Opinion in America* (New York, Harper, 1937), p. 109.

[7] Donald Davidson, *op. cit.*, pp. 360–362.

[8] Allen Tate, *Reactionary Essays on Poetry and Ideas* (New York, Charles Schibner's Sons, 1936), p. 155. Quotations used by permission of the publisher.

[9] Robert W. Stallman, "The New Criticism and the Southern Critics," *in* Allen Tate, ed. *A Southern Vanguard* (New York, Prentice-Hall, Inc., 1947), p. 21.

[10] John Crowe Ransom, *The World's Body* (New York, Charles Scribner's Sons, 1938), p. 31. Quotations used by permission of the publisher.

[11] Robert W. Stallman, *op. cit.*, p. 29.

[12] Allen Tate, *Reactionary Essays on Poetry and Ideas*, p. 19.

[13] *Ibid.*, p. 18.

CHAPTER 5.

[1] Vernon L. Parrington, *Main Currents in American Thought* (New York, Harcourt, 1930), I, 327.

[2] Constance Rourke, *The Roots of American Culture* (New York, Harcourt, 1942), p. 284.

[3] Philip Rahv, *The Discovery of Europe* (Boston, Houghton, Mifflin Co., 1947), p. xv. Quotations used by permission of the publisher.

[4] Waldo Frank, *Our America* (New York, Boni and Liveright, 1919), pp. 106–107.

[5] Merle Curti, *The Growth of American Thought* (New York, Harper and Brothers, 1943), pp. ix–x. Quotations used by permission of the publisher.

[6] Howard Mumford Jones, *Ideas in America* (Cambridge, Mass., Harvard, 1945), p. 125.

[7] *Ibid.*, pp. 177–179.

[8] George Santayana, *Three Philosophical Poets* (Cambridge, Mass., Harvard University Press, 1910), p. 196. Quotations used by permission of the publisher.

[9] D. H. Lawrence, "America, Listen to Your Own," *New Republic*, Vol. XXV, No. 315 (Dec. 15, 1920), pp. 68–69. Quotations used by permission of the *New Republic*.

[10] Ferner Nuhn, *The Wind Blew from the East* (New York, Harper and Bros., 1942), pp. 3–4. Quotations used by permission of the publisher.

[11] *Ibid.*, p. 76.

[12] *Ibid.*, p. 9

[13] *Ibid.*, pp. 7–8.

[14] Yvor Winters, *In Defense of Reason* (Denver, The University of Denver Press, 1947), p. 301. Quotations used by permission of Alan Swallow.

[15] Van Wyck Brooks, *New England: Indian Summer* (New York, Dutton, 1940; London, Dent, 1940), p. 140.

[16] Bernard DeVoto, *Mark Twain's America* (Boston, Little, Brown and Co., 1932), p. 190. Quotations used by permission of the author.

[17] F. O. Matthiessen, *American Renaissance* (New York, Oxford University Press, Inc., 1941), p. 474. Quotations used by permission of the publisher.

[18] Van Wyck Brooks, *The Flowering of New England* (New York, Dutton, 1936; London, Dent, 1936), p. 462.

[19] Malcolm Cowley, *Exile's Return* (New York, Viking, 1951), pp. 237–238.

[20] Van Wyck Brooks, *New England: Indian Summer*, pp. 502–503.

[21] Philip Rahv, *op. cit.*, p. xvii.

[22] Horace Gregory, "The Situation in American Writing," *in* William Phillips and Philip Rahv, eds., *The Partisan Reader* (New York, Dial Press, 1946), p. 613. Quotations used by permission of the publisher.

[23] Edna Kenton, "Henry James and the World," *in* F. W. Dupee, *The Question of Henry James* (New York, Holt, 1945), p. 135.

[24] Ferner Nuhn, *op. cit.*, p. 81.

Chapter 6.

[1] Newton Arvin, "The Democratic Tradition in American Letters," *in* H. Hart, ed., *The Writer in a Changing World* (New York, Equinox Cooperative Press, 1937), p. 38. Quotations used by permission of the author.

[2] F. O. Matthiessen, *American Renaissance* (New York, Oxford, 1941), p. xv.

[3] Stanley Edgar Hyman, *The Armed Vision* (New York, Alfred A. Knopf, Inc., 1948), p. 95. Quotations used by permission of the publisher.

[4] Granville Hicks, *The Great Tradition* (New York, The Macmillan Co., 1933), p. 328. Quotations used by permission of the author.

[5] Henry Seidel Canby, "The American Tradition in Literature," *Saturday Review of Literature*, Vol. XXII, No. 19 (Aug. 31, 1940), p. 16. Quotations used by permission of the *Saturday Review of Literature*.

[6] Alfred Kazin, *On Native Grounds* (New York, Reynal and Hitchcock, 1942), pp. 15–16.

[7] William Dean Howells, *Criticism and Fiction* (New York, Harper and Brothers, 1891), p. 8. Quotations used by permission of the publisher.

[8] Vernon L. Parrington, *Main Currents in American Thought* (New York, Harcourt, Brace, 1930), III, 243.

[9] John Dewey, *Art As Experience* (New York, Minton, Balch, 1934), p. 326. Quotations used by permission of G. P. Putnam's Sons.

[10] *Ibid.*, pp. 270–271.

[11] Karl Mannheim, *Man and Society* (New York, Harcourt, Brace and Co., Inc., 1940; London, Routledge and Kegan Paul Ltd., 1940), p. 79. Quotations used by permission of the publishers.

[12] Clement Greenberg, "Avant-Garde and Kitsch," *in* William Phillips and Philip Rahv, eds., *The Partisan Reader* (New York, Dial, 1946), pp. 380–382.

[13] Karl Mannheim, *op. cit.*, p. 100.

[14] William Phillips, "The Intellectuals' Tradition," *in* William Phillips and Philip Rahv, eds., *The Partisan Reader.*

[15] Herbert Read, *Art and Society* (New York, The Macmillan Co., 1937), p. 184.